ON LONELY ROADS . . .
IN THE MIDDLE OF CROWDED CITIES . . .
INEXPLICABLE, INCREDIBLE EVENTS
SHOW US A REALITY
THAT THE HARD FACTS CANNOT EXPLAIN . . .
BUT MIRACLES CAN.

• The barking phantom dog who appears out of the fog to take a family away from danger

• The silent hitchhiker who leads a doctor to a schoolbus crash . . . in which the hitchhiker has been killed

• The guardian angels who get a sick child to a hospital

• The vision of a twin that prevents a boy from boarding a doomed train

• The pupil who returns from the grave to save a teacher's life

• The religious medal that appears in time to save a Vietnam vet from suicide

FIND OUT ALL
THE SPELLBINDING DETAILS IN . . .

Miracles and Other Wonders

Other Bestselling Books
Authored by Charles E. Sellier

MIRACLES
AND
OTHER
WONDERS

≈≈≈

CHARLES E. SELLIER

A DELL BOOK

Published by
Dell Publishing
a division of
Bantam Doubleday Dell Publishing Group, Inc.
1540 Broadway
New York, New York 10036

ISBN: 0-440-21804-7

Printed in the United States of America

Dedication

To Governor Mike Leavitt and Sheriff Mike Spanos, the two "Mikes" in my life, who have helped me learn the benefits of helping others.

I am deeply grateful to both of them.

Acknowledgment

I want to express my deep appreciation to Joe Meier for his editorial assistance on this book. Both of us are in total awe of what our research uncovered.

Contents

PREFACE

IN SEARCH OF MIRACLES AND OTHER WONDERS

≈≈≈

I HAVE WRITTEN A NUMBER OF BOOKS, ALL OF THEM FIRMLY GROUNDED IN that great adventure we call "real life." For the past eighteen years I have devoted most of my efforts to the production of motion pictures, and whatever claim to fame I may have is largely attributable to that effort. It is also fair to say that the movies with which I have been associated have, for the most part, dealt with real people and real-life adventures. This book is no different.

When beginning the research for this book I assumed the greatest difficulty would be in finding people who were willing to share what are often very personal and private experiences. I was wrong. In fact, just the opposite is true. Once the word got out that we were seeking first-person accounts of true yet miraculous experiences, we quickly discovered that there are an amazing number of people not only willing but eager to share their own private miracles.

The greater task has become one of editing, for which I take sole responsibility. The criteria used for determining which stories to use and which to perhaps save for another time were purely subjective and no attempt was made to determine whether one story had more veracity than another. Instead I used the simple expedient of "going with" the depiction of those events that tugged a little more at my heartstrings, or perhaps did a little better job of demonstrating that "believing" is a bit of a miracle in and of itself, and one worth pursuing.

Upon completion of the selection process I discovered that the stories seemed to fall into five somewhat indistinct and rather general categories. They are:

MIRACLES THAT SAVE LIVES: While it is true that many of the stories have matters of life and death at their core, some seem to serve that single purpose more explicitly.

MIRACLES OF PERSONAL GROWTH: Frequently we came across stories of miraculous occurrences that have, as an ultimate result, the reshaping of people's lives to the extent they rise above themselves or become devoted to helping others.

MIRACLES OF FAMILY DEVOTION: Many of the stories we reviewed had as their central theme family togetherness, the prevention of a family's disintegration, or the saving of a particular family member.

MIRACLES THAT DEMONSTRATE TRANSCENDENT LOVE: In this category we found some of our most compelling events. There is no doubt that love can transcend all other obstacles, including death.

MIRACLES OF RELIGIOUS SIGNIFICANCE: It would be foolhardy to embark upon a work concerning miracles and attempt to overlook the significance of religious faith in the process. Indeed, the word *miracle* has its roots in the very substance of religion, as the events depicted in this category aptly demonstrate.

The marvelous events described in the following pages all happened. They are real events that took place in the lives of real people and in every case each seemingly isolated occurrence brought about a change not only in the lives of those directly involved but, like ripples on a pond, spread outward to touch the lives of others in a unique and marvelous way that truly made the world we live in a little better place. That unique aspect of these phenomena is one of the reasons I became convinced that stories such as these must be shared.

In a way you could say I came to this project by accident. Certainly I didn't just get up one bright summer morning and decide I was going to go out and discover my own miracle, but in fact that's what happened. An event took place in my life that persuaded me beyond any shadow of a doubt that such things are not only possible, they are, under the right circumstances, probable.

As you read through these pages you will encounter ordinary people doing ordinary things who are suddenly and inexplicably an integral part of something quite extraordinary, even miraculous. I know. It happened to me and my life was changed in ways I never would have imagined.

My purpose in writing this book (and producing the CBS television series of the same name) is to help everyone realize that miracles happen every day; that they serve a greater purpose than even the participants realize, and that far from being random events, unique to a particular type or group of people, miracles are the stuff of everyday life, intended to remind us that we are more, much more, than just a complex biological organism.

Let me begin by telling you of my own. . . .

Charles E. Sellier

PART I

MIRACLES THAT SAVE LIVES

≈≈≈

CHAPTER 1

MOUNTAIN
MIRACLE

≈≈≈

F OR MANY YEARS I HAVE MADE MY HOME IN PARK CITY, UTAH, AN OLD mining town turned ski resort located high in the Wasatch Mountains and most prominently known as the training center for the United States Olympic ski team. The crisp, cold winters, the mild springs and summers, and the blazing falls that splash a kaleidoscope of colors across the Wasatch Mountains suit me perfectly. Of course, the fact that Park City is just a short, scenic drive down Parley's Canyon to Salt Lake City is a plus, too, since that's where Sun International Pictures, Inc., my motion-picture production company, is located.

Fifteen years ago I decided I wanted to give something back to the community that afforded myself and my family so much enjoyment. I became a certified police officer for the state of Utah and volunteered my services to the Wasatch County sheriff's office. Over the past fifteen years I have gone out on many patrols, but none of them was more significant than the one I am going to tell you about.

Just southeast of Park City, not more than fifteen miles, lies the small farming community of Heber City. Before Park City became a major international ski resort and tourist mecca, Heber City was the hub of activity for this area. It is still the political center of Wasatch County and is home to all county government offices, including the sheriff's department.

Because my duties as a volunteer deputy sheriff were so integral to the events that transpired that day, it's important to give you some idea of the area I was required to serve. Heber City—calling it a "city" is really a bit extravagant—serves as a gateway to a number of recreational areas, among them Strawberry and Deer Creek reservoirs and the many lakes and campgrounds of the Uinta Mountains. It was my job to run the main roads leading into and out of these areas, assist the Heber City officers if necessary, and be available for any emergencies that might arise in and around a primary patrol area of some forty-five square miles.

The weekend in question just happened to be the Fourth of July weekend. Typically on the Fourth of July in this part of the world things are pretty quiet. The big celebrations take place in Provo or Salt Lake and the Wasatch County sheriff's office was principally involved with making sure the seemingly endless line of boats and campers got to Strawberry, Deer Creek, or the many campgrounds of the Uintas.

Typically, too, the regular deputies put in for time off on that weekend, and that meant that those of us who were volunteers got the call.

It may be self-evident—after all, a person is not likely to do something voluntarily for over fifteen years if it isn't enjoyable—but I want to make it very clear: I relished the time I spent working for the people of the county. I looked forward to the phone call that gave me those assignments, and only the most pressing demands of my business would keep me from accepting anytime that I was asked to come on duty.

I looked forward to it because invariably something would happen that gave me an opportunity to help someone in need. It may have just been providing a gallon of coolant to some guy trying to pull a boat up Daniels Canyon with a pickup truck that had an engine half the size of the one in his boat, or it might have been staying with an accident victim until an ambulance arrived, but whatever it was, for me it was satisfying.

As things worked out on this particular Fourth of July weekend, I was the only deputy working. All of the full-time deputies had asked for and received holiday leave.

Even at that it was a quiet patrol; I hadn't heard any traffic on the radio for hours. The patrol routes we followed were well defined and I found myself beginning to wonder how many times I could cover the valley in one day. Still, an occasional wave from a friendly passerby and the sense that I was available, "just in case," made it all worthwhile.

My vehicle was a four-wheel-drive Ford Bronco, dark brown and cream colored, complete with sheriff markings and police lights and sirens. It was clearly visible along the main routes in and out of town and I began to feel like visibility might be the sum and substance of my contribution for the day.

Suddenly, late in the afternoon, the radio crackled to life. Dispatch had a report of an accident with injuries near Deer Creek Reservoir. I instructed the dispatcher to roll an ambulance and headed the Bronco down toward Provo Canyon, lights and sirens going full blast. It turned out to be a fairly standard auto accident, a few cuts and bruises but no fatalities. I was in the process of wrapping up when the radio grabbed my attention again.

"L-four . . . L-four, are you where you can hear me? Over."

I reached into the car and lifted the microphone from its hook. "This is L-four. What's up? Over."

"If you can wrap that up we just got a call from the Other End. Some guy's gone nuts and he's taking the place apart. Over."

"Just need a signature here and I'm on my way. L-four clear."

I quickly finished up at the accident scene, turned the vehicle around, and headed back toward Heber City. The Other End was a bar, literally on the other end of town. To be more precise, the north end. It was, in fact, the last establishment you passed before the speed-limit change that signaled open highway all the way to Kimball Junction and the turnoff to Park City.

Among its other charms Heber City is very much like a small section of the Swiss Alps, magically transported to this small valley between the Wasatch and the Uinta mountains. On the west side of the valley and just a mile or two north of my destination is an area called Midway, a township that consists mostly of summer homes and cabins. A state-owned and -operated golf course a mile or two west of most of the homesites is the centerpiece of what is known as Wasatch State Park. Farther east, closer to the homes but still outside the park boundaries, a small resort that boasts a natural hot-spring swimming pool offers yet another diversion.

It is a quiet area, except for holiday weekends, and because most of it is designated a state park it was not part of our normal patrol route. Patrols were mostly left up to the park rangers.

Given the fact that I was heading for a situation that could occupy my time for a couple of hours, it was disconcerting for me to suddenly realize I was not thinking about the bar or its problem. Instead, for some inexplicable reason, my attention was riveted on a section of the park northwest of the golf course. I mentally calculated it to be somewhere close to the mouth of a small canyon called Guardsman Pass.

Fire is sometimes a problem up there, but I could see no telltale wisp of smoke or anything else that could give me a clue as to what might be out of place. Still, the feeling was very unsettling. I couldn't get my mind back to the business at hand. Even as I pulled up in front of the bar and climbed out of the vehicle I stopped to take one more look at that spot on the mountainside.

A city officer was already there by the time I arrived, and between the two of us we quickly got things quieted down and the city officer hustled the offender off to jail. I looked at my watch. It was the time of day when traffic coming down the canyon from Strawberry Reservoir begins to get clogged with fishermen coming off the lake. The highways are two lane and as long as everyone keeps moving there isn't much of a problem, but the guy who overheats or blows a tire or runs out of gas can back cars and trailers up for miles. My normal routine should have been to start working the main routes up through Daniels Canyon and back down through Provo Canyon, but for some reason I was compelled to focus on that area of the mountain just beyond Midway once again.

What was wrong up there? What was it about that spot on the mountain that bothered me? And why should I be concerned? It wasn't part of my patrol area.

As I climbed back into the Bronco I tried to shake the feeling. My common sense told me there was nothing there and I was much more likely to be needed back toward the south end of the valley. Nevertheless, when I nosed the police car up to the highway with my head and all my common sense telling me to turn right, my hand dropped the turn signal down to the "left" position and I turned north toward the Midway road.

There was still nothing to see, but my eyes kept returning to the same spot at the base of the canyon. It was not, I decided, Guardsman Pass after all. Guardsman was an area I knew very well and the closer I got the more I realized I was being drawn toward a canyon farther to the west known as Snake Creek. It was probably beyond the park boundaries and an area in which I had never been.

I remember thinking it was fortunate that the Bronco had four-wheel drive, since I didn't even know if a road cut through that area. And there was something else. Now that I had quit struggling with the decision of whether or not to check it out, my feelings began to take on a sense of urgency.

It was a typical holiday weekend in Midway. The resort swimming pool always attracted a number of people. Most of the homes in the area appeared to be bustling with activity, and the golf course was as busy as I'd ever seen it. As I drove up through the area I stopped and spoke with a few people, asked them if everything was all right, if they were aware of any problems anywhere, but everyone seemed to be having a good time and I received no information that could account for my growing conviction that something was terribly wrong.

I continued on toward the spot that had first absorbed my interest from back on the highway. Soon I was well past the golf course and on past the turnoff to Guardsman Pass. There was still blacktop under the wheels but the road had narrowed to the minimum two-lane width and was obviously not very high on the maintenance priority list. I was now in an area that was unfamiliar, but as long as the road took me in the general direction of that small canyon I kept the Bronco moving north and west.

From time to time it occurred to me that I'd have a hard time explaining to the dispatcher why I was here if she happened to call me, but those were fleeting thoughts and not nearly compelling enough to make me turn the vehicle around.

Suddenly the paved road veered away to the south. I figured I must be at the very edge of the state park or maybe even beyond its bounds. It wasn't likely that there would be any park rangers up here, in fact it wasn't likely that anyone would be up here. I had passed the last marked campground several miles back. Once again my head tried to take over. I should get back to my primary patrol area. But even as those thoughts went through my mind I looked out over the hood and saw, still heading up to the northwest, the faint hint of an old mining road that looked as if maybe, sometime in the distant past, a vehicle might have gone that way. I dropped the transmission into low gear and eased into the weed- and grass-filled tracks.

This was not, I told myself for the umpteenth time, the place for the only on-duty deputy in the Wasatch County Sheriff's Department to be on the Fourth of July weekend, but, I could not turn back.

I had gone a few hundred yards up this road when it suddenly took a sharp turn to the left and dropped down along the side of the hill. I took the turn cautiously, scanning the rocks and sagebrush that were the only things in my line of sight. Then the nose of the Bronco dipped down and I saw them. Two elderly people, a man and a woman, sprawled in the road in front of me. They were clearly hurt, arms and legs bent at strange angles. The woman was closest to me and I could see blood trickling down her cheek. My heart jumped inside of me as I realized neither of them was moving.

Instinctively I grabbed the microphone on my radio and fired a message to dispatch. I gave them my location as best I could and requested an ambulance, then pulled the first-aid kit from its holder, jumped out of the rig, and ran to the woman. I judged her to be at least eighty years of age and I couldn't imagine what in the world could bring a couple that old to such a remote spot, and alone.

As I began to check the woman for a pulse and broken bones, she started to come around.

"Please," she said, "go to my husband. Help him. He doesn't deserve to die like this. He just wanted to show me he could be young again."

Fighting back the emotion her selfless request brought to the surface, I wrapped her in a blanket and propped her legs up to protect against shock and then proceeded to the elderly man. He was, I learned later, eighty-four years old, and badly hurt. He had several broken bones and was bleeding. He would need much more help than I could give him.

Just about that time a park ranger who had heard my call for assistance pulled in behind the Bronco, and not far behind him was the ambulance I had asked for. I remember wondering how they could have arrived so fast, but at the moment I was just thankful they were there.

The ambulance crew immediately went to work on the old man, so I went back to the woman to try and offer what comfort I could. It was then that I saw the dirt bike lying on its side about twenty yards off the trail.

The woman was unable to move but didn't seem to have any life-threatening injuries, and by now she was fully aware of what was going on. She told me they had been invited to spend the holiday at their son's cabin. The other members of the family had all gone off to participate in some other activity, leaving Grandma and Grandpa to enjoy the cabin and its amenities by themselves. Her husband, she said, spotted the dirt bike and decided it would be fun to go for a ride.

"What do you say?" he asked her. "Let's give it one last fling. Let's have a little fun one more time."

"It seemed," she said, "like such a golden moment between us that I didn't have the heart to tell him no."

They had hopped on the dirt bike together and proceeded down the road, not realizing, in the joy of the moment, just how far they had gone. Everything was going well and when they came to this old mining road they had turned onto it full of confidence. After all, a dirt bike was for riding on dirt. It was when they came to the sharp turn and the road suddenly fell away downhill that her husband had lost control.

At first she had tried to get to her husband but something prevented her from even crawling toward him. She called out and when there was no response her heart sank and for a few moments, she told me, she felt nothing but despair. But then she heard a sound, a slight moan, and she knew he was alive.

"I turned to God," she said, "and told Him He needed to send us some help. He couldn't let us die like this, it wouldn't be fair."

She didn't know how long she had prayed before she lost consciousness or how long they had been lying there before she felt my hand on her wrist, but she never doubted for a moment, she told me, that someone would come.

"For a few minutes," she said softly, "riding up the road on that motorbike, I had my youthful husband back. I knew God wouldn't let us die like this," she added. "I knew He would send someone."

There had been something about the way she greeted me when she first opened her eyes that had struck me as a little bit odd, but I really hadn't been able to put my finger on it. As she concluded her story I suddenly realized what it was. She had not been the least bit surprised to see me. She had simply opened her eyes and begun giving me instructions.

The medics did what they could for them and called in a Life Flight helicopter to take them to a hospital. One of the medics told me that if I hadn't shown up both of them would surely have died. It was late in the afternoon and temperatures drop rapidly in these high mountain valleys once the sun disappears. More importantly, neither of them could move and they were on a road that was seldom if ever used. If I hadn't "happened by," he said, their fate would have been sealed.

Later, back at the office, Sheriff Spanos asked me what in the world had possessed me to go up into that remote area. The only answer I could give was simply that there was a spot on the mountain that had been calling to me all afternoon. I knew the sheriff to be a religious man and it did not go unnoticed that he didn't seem to be surprised either. He just smiled and said, "Good job."

In retrospect I think the woman had a better answer than I did. "He would send someone," she had told me. And the more I think about it the more convinced I am that I was indeed sent to that spot.

The feelings that washed over me as I watched the old couple being loaded onto the helicopter, knowing they would both be all right, were nothing short of exhilarating. I wanted to shout, to give somebody a high five, to spike the ball. At that moment there wasn't anyplace on earth that I would rather have been than on that remote mountain road.

As the helicopter lifted off I turned my attention back to the paramedics. The fact that they had appeared on the scene so soon after my call had only seemed curious at first, but the more I thought about it the more I realized it should have taken a half an hour or more to get an ambulance up there. And a four-wheel-drive ambulance at that—given a choice most of the paramedics will choose the bigger and more elaborately equipped units.

Strangely enough, about an hour before my call someone at the golf course had requested an ambulance. The dispatcher had beeped the volunteers and the two men standing there with me had responded. For some reason they had decided to take the smaller, four-wheel-drive unit.

It turned out to be a false call. No one at the golf course needed an ambulance. When I put in my call the ambulance was just pulling out of the golf-course parking lot a few miles away. All they had to do was turn right instead of left and they were able to respond to my call in just a matter of minutes.

"And what were you doing up here?" I asked the park ranger.

"I don't know," he said, "I usually don't come up this far till deer season, but I thought I'd check out the campgrounds and heard your call."

As a working member of the media I know that we all live in a great, fluctuating, electromagnetic soup. We take our radios and TVs to the beach or up into the mountains or out into the desert, and when we flip the switch we simply expect something to be there, and it is. That's because there are people pumping signals into the electromagnetic spectrum. These signals are always there, surrounding us with sounds and images most of us never see or hear. We can't see these signals or touch them, we can't taste them or feel them, but they're present just the same and all it takes to bring them to life is for someone, anyone, to turn on the proper receiver.

I began to wonder if maybe we aren't surrounded by another "communication system" as well, one that puts us in touch with each other in our most desperate hour of need.

Here was a woman, alone and hurt, reaching out to her God in selfless prayer, asking Him to send someone to help her husband. Fifteen miles away a movie producer and part-time volunteer police officer, who was a bit of a stranger to prayer, received . . . what? . . . a message? . . . to go to a spot on the mountain where he had never been and had no business being. This officer, following instincts that were at war with his intellect, suddenly arrived on the scene with the means to answer her prayers. The cynic may call it a coincidence, but I can assure you that woman knows differently.

There is no doubt in my mind that I was used as the instrument of answering her prayers. There was nothing haphazard or coincidental about the way the events of this rescue came about. I was compelled to go to that particular spot. The sense of urgency that moved me up that mountain road is still vivid in my memory today and the resulting experience changed my life forever. It changed the way I think and feel about our relationship as human beings and the responsibilities we all share to be there for one another, regardless of the circumstances.

This experience brought home to me the realization that sooner or later we all have an opportunity to help others. In my own mind it goes much deeper than just being in the right place at the right time. It goes back fifteen years to the day I made the decision to be a volunteer officer, it goes to the very reasons for making that decision. I can tell you today that if in my entire fifteen years of service nothing else of any note had taken place, the feelings, the understanding, that came to me that Fourth of July afternoon would still have made it all worthwhile.

And the more I thought about it the more I realized this experience could not possibly be unique to me. I decided to do some investigating and see if there weren't others with similar experiences. If there were, perhaps I could persuade them to share those experiences.

Do I believe the things in this book actually happened? Do I believe in miracles? The truth is my own experiences have convinced me that it wouldn't be much of a world without them.

In largely the same way that I was drawn to that spot on the mountain, I have been drawn back to this book and the television series upon which it is based. I can't escape the idea that by sharing some of the miracles that take place every day all around us we can perhaps create a greater miracle: the miracle of hope and of the understanding that no matter how difficult things may become, there are unseen forces that shape our lives, bring hope to the hopeless, and remind us that after all is said and done, it is through helping one another that we achieve the most memorable and lasting rewards.

Now you know why I believe in miracles and why I think it's important that this book be written. And I'm sure you'll agree that the events that appear to have no other purpose than the miraculous saving of a life get our most immediate and undivided attention. So let's begin our journey through the world of *Miracles and Other Wonders* by examining a few of these remarkable events.

Oh! Remember that "electromagnetic soup" I told you about earlier? The idea that we are constantly surrounded by signals seeking the proper receiver? That concept includes such seemingly inconsequential devices as a CB or citizens band radio. And it includes the idea that the consequence of these signals can reach across the vast expanse of time as well as space. Keep that in mind as we begin to unfold . . . .

CHAPTER 2

THE
BARNEY MAIZ
STORY

≈≈≈

Barney Maiz was black, a child of the Depression and of the Chicago ghetto. But Barney Maiz was made of different stuff. He determined that not only was he going to escape the wretched poverty that had trapped most of the people he grew up with, he was going to make certain he would never have to face those circumstances again.

As a young man working on the loading dock of a local trucking firm, he had learned the intricacies of moving the big eighteen-wheelers around the yard. At first it was just moving the empties away from the dock or backing one of the long-haul rigs into position to be unloaded, but one day Barney climbed up into the cab and decided that was where he belonged.

Over the next several years Barney acquired a reputation for dependability, and a rig of his own. And somewhere along the way he met Cecily and they were married. When she became pregnant with their first son they loaded all their possessions into Barney's truck and headed west. They didn't stop until they got to Montana.

In most cities in Montana it's still possible to find a comfortable home on a full acre of ground and still be living in what most folks call the "suburbs." Barney and Cecily had found just such a place. Leonard, now a strapping seventeen-year-old, was born here, so was his fifteen-year-old sister, Kirsten, and just seven years ago Bobby had come along. They were children of the high mountains and open spaces with no inkling of what their father and mother had left behind.

But Barney couldn't forget the poverty that had shaped his early life, and even though his twenty-hour days and long-haul bonuses had made it possible for them to burn the mortgage several years ago, he was still compelled to take on every load and push for every bonus. This meant he was spending an average of twenty days out of every month pounding up and down the road. Leonard and Kirsten had given up the idea of ever seeing him at any of their school functions and Bobby had grown up thinking he was just some guy who stopped by once in a while for a bed and a bath.

In his unremitting drive to give his family everything they could ever want, Barney was denying them the one thing they wanted most, a husband and father.

Barney didn't understand any of this, of course; he was simply irritated by the distance he could feel opening up between himself and his family. Distance was something Barney understood very well. His entire life was spent trying to overcome the loneliness that crept into his bones as he negotiated the vast distances between the cities and towns of the western United States. Now he was beginning to sense the same loneliness on his brief stopovers at home, and he lashed out against it in complete frustration. Barney, without knowing why, was in danger of losing the very thing he was working so hard to protect.

It was late summer and Barney had been home for two days without a call. He told himself he was glad to be there, but petty bickering with his son and daughter and the nagging fear that he was somehow losing money by not being on the road kept him on edge. When the phone finally rang with an offer for a bonus run from Helena to Spokane, everyone, including Barney, heaved a sigh of relief.

He had barely hung up the phone before Kirsten was standing in the hallway handing him the travel bag he always kept packed and ready to go. There was an awkward silence as he took it and turned to leave.

"Leonard, come and help me check the rig," he said quietly.

The two of them walked outside in silence. Barney tossed his bag into the sleeper and brought out a couple of miniature baseball bats.

"You take that side," he told Leonard, handing him one of the bats. Then he began giving each of the huge tires a resounding whack to make sure it was up to pressure.

It was a well-practiced routine, and they went about it in silence. They checked the air lines to the trailer brakes, the hydraulic-system connections, and made sure the running lights were clean and the taillights and turn signals clear of mud. Finally Barney handed the key to his son and told him to go ahead and fire it up.

There had been a time, Barney was sure, when starting the huge engine was the highlight of Leonard's life. Now he approached it as if it was just another chore.

A great belch of black smoke broke from the exhaust as the engine roared to life. Leonard climbed down without a word.

"Thanks, son. I appreciate your help."

"Sure." Leonard watched his dad climb up into the cab, then added, "You're gonna miss the first day of football practice again."

"What?"

"I'm the halfback, remember? You said you'd come and watch us practice."

"Oh, yeah." Barney had forgotten all about it. "Well, maybe I can catch a practice next week."

"Dad"—Leonard's voice was full of anger—"I'm a senior. I've been on the team for three years and you haven't seen a game or a practice. Who do you think you're kidding?"

Leonard turned and stomped past his mother and slammed the door behind him. Cecily walked over to the cab and looked up at her husband. "He thinks you don't care about him," she shouted against the roar of the engine.

"What's he think I'm doin' this for?" Barney shouted angrily. Then he saw the concern on Cecily's face. Slowly he climbed down out of the rig and gathered her in his arms.

"It'll be all right," he said, but somewhere deep down he shared her concern.

"He thinks you're doing it just so you won't have to stay home with us."

"But that's stupid," Barney replied, his frustration beginning to rise, "we need the money."

"Do we?" The question caught Barney completely by surprise.

"You know we do. What if the truck breaks down? What if the furnace goes on the fritz like it did last year? What if—"

"What if you lose contact with your son?" Cecily interrupted.

Barney's mouth snapped shut. He kissed Cecily on the cheek and climbed back up into the cab of the truck. They'd discuss it some more when he got back.

Barney picked up the load in Helena and turned his rig up the highway toward Spokane. Almost automatically he reached up and flipped on the CB, mounted within easy reach of his right hand. Like all truckers Barney had learned to cure the loneliness of these long hauls by talking to other drivers on the highway or sometimes just listening in on the never-ending conversation.

He was three, maybe four hours out of Helena when the radio suddenly went dead. Barney fiddled with the gain and the squelch but nothing came from the tinny speaker but silence. It was surprising but not too unsettling. After all, he was traveling a part of the country where there was nothing but miles and miles of miles and miles. It was vaguely disturbing that he couldn't remember the last time he hadn't been able to pick up something on one of the 40 channels the CB was capable of receiving.

Barney settled back in his seat, strangely comfortable in the silence. He thought about turning on the regular radio to see if maybe he could pick up a talk show or something, but quickly decided against it. He wasn't sleepy and he was enjoying the quiet.

During the next half hour Barney reached up and checked his CB two or three times just out of habit. He walked through the channels but found nothing, and he was beginning to think maybe the thing had just died on him in spite of the fact that all of the indicator lights told him it was working. He flipped it back to channel 19, the channel most truckers monitor, and gave his full attention to the road ahead of him.

Suddenly the CB snapped to life. That in itself wasn't too surprising, but the message was.

"Help me! Somebody, please help me."

Barney grabbed the mike from its holder and keyed the transmitter. "Say again, man. If you got trouble, come on back."

There was a brief silence, then Barney heard the same voice again. It sounded weak and distant.

"In a very bad way. Heart attack. Car damaged. Can't hang on much longer."

Barney keyed the mike once again: "Anybody out there picking up this distress call? This guy sounds like he's got big trouble. Anybody out there? Come back."

He released the transmit button and waited anxiously, but the only thing on the air was the plea for help.

"Need help badly. Please, somebody . . . getting very cold, can't move."

Barney knew that any delay could cost him his early-delivery bonus. He was on a tight schedule that would be tough to make under the best of circumstances, but there just didn't seem to be another driver out there to whom he could hand this call.

"What's your twenty, man?" Barney snapped. "Where are you? Looks like I'm all the help you're gonna get, so you better come on back."

Barney had to turn up the volume to hear what was becoming an almost whispered message: "Old deserted gas station," the voice murmured. "County Road Twenty-six . . . ten miles north of the interstate."

"Oh, great," Barney said out loud as he slapped the steering wheel. "I passed that turnoff five miles back. Bye bye, bonus."

It took a few more minutes to find a spot wide enough to turn his rig around, but soon Barney was on the other side of the highway looking for the turnoff to County Road 26. The next twenty minutes were the longest of his life.

At last the road sign popped into his headlights and he swung the big eighteen-wheeler onto the county road. He punched up his bright lights and centered the spotlight on top of his cab to a point about fifty yards ahead of his high beam and onto the right shoulder of the road. There were still no other voices on his CB.

Finally he saw it. A late-model sedan had missed a curve and slid up against the old pump of an abandoned gas station. Barney pulled to a stop with the tractor positioned so that his lights flooded the area. He grabbed a couple of blankets from the sleeper and ran over to the car.

The driver, a well-dressed man, probably in his mid-fifties, was sitting behind the wheel, his head slumped forward on his chest. The window on the driver's side was partially rolled down and the man inside tried to raise his head as Barney approached.

"My nitro pills . . . in my bag." He gasped and his head slumped forward again.

Quickly Barney rummaged through the bag and found a small bottle labeled NITROGLYCERIN. He spread the blankets on the ground, then carefully opened the car door, brought the man out, and laid him in a full reclining position.

"The pills," the man whispered. "Put one under my tongue."

Barney did as he was instructed and within seconds the man's breathing became less labored.

With the man apparently out of immediate danger Barney rushed back to his truck. This guy was going to need more help than he could give him, and his only link to the rest of the world was his CB.

To his surprise, when Barney climbed back up into the cab his radio was alive with traffic.

"Well, I'll be . . ." he muttered, then flipped down to channel 9, the channel most law enforcement and emergency units monitor, and broke in.

"Breaker nine . . . breaker nine. I have a man in bad trouble near the old gas station on County Road Twenty-six. Looks like a heart attack. I need some help. Come back."

Barney let go of the mike switch and held his breath. Almost immediately the reply came back.

"This is Pike County Deputy Orwell. I copy. I'm calling for an ambulance."

Barney just stared at the CB for a moment, then hung the mike back on its carrier and rushed back to the man lying in the road. By the time the ambulance arrived along with Deputy Orwell, the man's breathing had returned to normal and there was a little bit of color coming back to his face.

"How'd you find him way out here?" Deputy Orwell asked. "Don't see many big rigs on these county roads."

"Oh, I was up on the interstate," Barney replied. "I just happened to pick up his distress call on my CB. He told me where he was and I came on back here."

The deputy made his way over to the man's car while Barney chatted with the ambulance driver. They wanted to know what he had done, how many pills he had given the man, and that sort of thing. Satisfied, they loaded their patient into the ambulance, thanked Barney, and drove off.

Barney had turned to get back in his truck when the deputy stopped him.

"Hey, man, you jerkin' my chain or what?"

Barney was puzzled. "What do you mean?" he asked.

"Well, I don't know what kind of a game you're playin' here," the deputy replied, "but there ain't no CB in that car."

"Whaaaat!" Barney hurried over to the car, still illuminated in the lights from his truck. He ducked inside, looked under the dashboard, the seats, he even checked the trunk. The deputy was right. There was no CB of any kind in that car.

The miles to his destination in Spokane and back home again were filled with consternation. Barney had heard the voice on his CB, he was sure of it. But there was no arguing the fact that there had been no CB in the man's car. And what of the sudden and complete silence on his radio before he heard the message? He had considered it just a little bit odd at the time, but now in retrospect it seemed almost spooky.

It occurred to him that with other traffic on the CB he probably wouldn't have heard the call for help. Somehow the two things had to be tied together. And the fact was, he had followed the man's instructions and found him exactly where he said he would be. It couldn't have been his imagination or just a happy coincidence. Somebody was trying to tell him something, he was sure of it.

Barney Maiz returned home with a heightened sense of his own mortality and a much keener awareness of the things that were most important in his life. He began to spend less and less time on the road, took more local hauls, and made sure he didn't accept jobs that would put him on the road when Leonard suited up for a game or Kirsten got a starring role in the school play. He even found time to help Leonard rebuild a '67 Mustang they found in old man Miller's barn.

They were a family now, a real family, and Barney was sure he knew the reason it had been his CB that received that distress call in the middle of the night. Someone besides the man in the car had sent him a message that night, and he was awfully glad he had been tuned in.

But that was not the end of it.

There was an even more astonishing chapter yet to be written.

Barney kept his family the center of his life from that point on, but little Bobby was grown up and away at college before he finally sold his rig and told Cecily that they were now officially retired.

It had been a dozen years since that fateful night and Barney's attention had turned to other things, like discovering new fishing waters with his good friend Mike DeSalvo.

A few years earlier Mike had talked Barney into taking a fishing trip with him to the trout streams of the White Mountain Apache reservation on the New Mexico border. Barney had fallen in love with the wild and beautiful country that is arguably some of the most spectacular in the entire Southwest. Not only that—the fishing was great as well.

Their trip to White Mountain had become an annual affair and this year Gray Hawk, their Apache guide, had promised to take them to a stream no one ever fished. Gray Hawk assured them they would have it all to themselves.

Several miles up into the back country Barney began to understand just why it was that nobody ever fished this particular stream. It was a long, arduous hike and the pack he was carrying, full of food and fishing gear, wasn't making it any easier. At first he was just irritated by the fact that he had to keep stopping to catch his breath, but he was soon falling farther and farther behind. Now he looked up ahead at Mike and Gray Hawk and realized his vision was blurry and the frequent stops weren't enough to help him get his breath back.

"Mike," he shouted, letting the pack slide from his shoulders, "I don't think I'm gonna make it."

Gray Hawk got to Barney's side just about the time he slumped to his knees. His energy was completely gone and his left arm was beginning to feel numb. Gray Hawk was an experienced guide and immediately recognized the symptoms of a heart attack.

"Give me a hand, Mike." Gray Hawk was already lifting Barney up so they could hold him between them. "We'll have to get him to the village about a mile from here."

"Do they have a doctor there?" Mike asked, moving in and supporting Barney on the opposite side.

"Sometimes," Gray Hawk replied.

"Sometimes?" It was not the encouraging reply either Mike or Barney had hoped for, but on the other hand, where else could they go?

What Gray Hawk didn't tell them was that the village was served by a traveling nurse who came in only once a month. She always pulled a small trailer that, in addition to her living quarters, contained a good supply of various kinds of medical supplies and some modern equipment. Gray Hawk felt certain that if she was there she would be able to help Barney. The question was, would she be there?

By the time they were in sight of the village Barney's strength had gone. He was barely conscious and Mike and Gray Hawk were literally carrying him. As they cleared a small stand of trees near the edge of the village Gray Hawk broke into a broad smile. The nurse's trailer stood out conspicuously against the scattered houses of the village.

"We're in luck," he said softly. "She's here."

"Hey, ya hear that Barney, boy?" Mike grunted. "You're gonna be all right."

Lying on a bed in one of the homes, drifting in and out of consciousness, Barney Maiz was oblivious to the conversation that was going on around him.

Mercedes Erlich Conway was a competent and dedicated medical practitioner, but the very low blood pressure and irregular heart rhythm told her that Barney had suffered a myocardial infarction, a condition that was beyond her expertise.

"Your friend," she said to Mike, "may be the luckiest man on the planet."

"Right now he don't look so lucky," Mike replied sadly.

"Wait here," she said, turning to go. "My father is a heart specialist. He was at my home visiting when it came time for me to come out here. For some reason he decided to come along. I'll get him and be right back."

A few minutes later Dr. Erlich came through the door carrying a portable monitor and oxygen equipment. He was an older man, enjoying the early years of his retirement with a visit to his daughter, but right now he was all business. Barney's condition was critical, and even with a specialist at his side it was going to be close.

The conversation that went on between Dr. Erlich and his daughter as they worked feverishly to stabilize Barney's heart rate was mostly

Greek to Mike and Gray Hawk, but they understood the smile on the doctor's face when the monitor began to show a steady and regular heartbeat.

"I think we've got him, Sis," Dr. Erlich said to his daughter. Then, turning to Mike and Gray Hawk, he added, "You boys got him here just in the nick of time. I think he's going to be all right."

Finding a cardiologist in the middle of an Indian reservation at the precise moment one was needed would be miracle enough for any story, but there was still one more astonishing revelation to come.

By the next morning Barney was resting comfortably, pulse and breathing almost back to normal. Dr. Erlich came in early, checked his vital signs, then shut off the oxygen and removed the mask from Barney's face. Just at that moment his daughter came through the door.

"How's he doing?" she asked cheerily.

"He's doing just fine," Dr. Erlich replied, turning back to look at his patient. "I think he may have . . ."

The sentence trailed off to silence as he stared at Barney, lying quietly in the bed.

"What is it, Dad?" Mercedes was suddenly concerned.

"I know him. I know this man."

"But how? I mean he's—"

At that instant Barney opened his eyes and for a moment thought he must be living in a dream. He was looking into the face of the man whose life he had saved so many years before. Older to be sure, but it was the same man, there could be no doubt about that.

"Am I awake?" Barney asked dazedly.

"Indeed you are," the doctor answered, then quickly added, "Do you know me?"

Some of the cobwebs were beginning to shake loose and Barney replied, "Yes, sir, I believe I do. You look very much like a man I helped on the highway one time."

Dr. Erlich reached down and grasped Barney's hand. "I have never forgotten your face," Dr. Erlich said, "but I never knew your name or how you came to find me that night."

Barney smiled. "I don't know yours either," he said.

"I'm Dr. Erlich, Dr. Curtis Erlich. Your friends brought you here last night with a nasty heart attack. You gave us quite a time."

"Well, then, I guess we're even, Doc, 'cause you gave me quite a time a few years back too."

"Yes, I remember. I've thought about that night many times. I can't tell you how grateful I am that you stopped to help me. Some of my most notable work was done after I recovered from that accident."

"Do you own a CB radio, Doc?" Barney asked, a note of seriousness in his voice.

"No, I don't. I've never had one."

"You should get one," Barney said with a smile. "They come in mighty handy."

The miracle of the CB message Barney Maiz heard on a lonely highway in Montana had come full circle. By saving a stranger's life on a lonely county road he had, literally and miraculously, saved his own.

CHAPTER 3

SNOWDRIFTS
AND DREAMS

≈≈≈

ELTON MCCABE IS A FOURTH-GENERATION ARIZONA CATTLEMAN. HIS six-hundred-acre spread in Coconino County was homesteaded by his great-grandfather. His grandfather had taken him out when he was barely big enough to sit on a horse and shown him the boundaries of their land, and his father had chosen to come back and work the ranch rather than pursue a master's degree.

"Mac," as just about everyone within shootin' distance called him, was truly born to the land. His teenage son, Elton junior, was of a like mind and never complained about long hours in the saddle or seven-day workweeks. More importantly, the McCabes had found that special rapport that comes from love, trust, and sharing the load.

As a matter of fact, love, trust, and sharing the load was a way of life for the whole McCabe family. Neighbors for miles around knew they could always count on the McCabes in time of need. There was hardly a family in Coconino County that couldn't tell a story about Mac and his boy pitching in to help them when they were in trouble.

Elton McCabe didn't think much about it, though. To him it was just the way things had always been, the way things were supposed to be. You pulled your neighbor's ox out of the mire and you just sort of expected he'd do the same for you.

Mrs. McCabe was part and parcel of the same tradition, and except for the fact that her husband didn't get nearly as excited about going to church as he did about going to the cattle auction, she thought her life was just about perfect.

≈

Down in Phoenix a young man by the name of Davey Hartley was getting ready for his trip to camp. The kind of life that Junior McCabe lived every day was a once-a-year dream for Davey, and he looked forward to it eagerly. Davey was just nine years old, and the excitement of going to Camp Firebird, high in the mountains of Coconino County, was almost more than he could contain. The YMCA had sponsored this camping trip for years. Charlie and Luretta Hartley were sure their boy would be in good hands.

There was one little thing that bothered them, however. Nothing major, really, just a little bit disconcerting. The past few mornings Davey had told his parents about a dream he'd been having almost every night. In his dream he was lying flat on his back in the snow while more snow slowly covered him up. He could hear someone calling his name and then he would see a man on a horse. He tried to call out to the man but couldn't make any sound. He always woke up trying to answer.

Mrs. Hartley sort of suggested one day that maybe Davey should think about not going to camp this year, but Davey didn't like that idea at all. He didn't tell his mom he didn't like the idea, he just ignored it altogether.

When the van that was to take him and the other boys to camp slowed to a stop in front of the house, Davey was out the door with his backpack before the driver had time to honk. His mother had to rush out with his coat or they would have driven off without it.

Back at the McCabe Ranch Mac and Junior were putting in some long days. A storm was building up over the Kaibab, and Mac's experience told him it could be a big one. It was still early in the year and the McCabes, as well as the other ranchers, still had cattle out on the open range. That meant a big loss if they couldn't bring them in.

Slowly but surely they had been able to round up most of the herd and at least get them down out of the high country where hay could be trucked to them if need be. But that, along with getting the stacks covered and all of the other livestock sheltered, had taken its toll on the two men. Preparing a ranch for winter is a two- or three-week process, not two days, and every night it was long after dark before they got into the house for supper and a chance to shake the cold from their bones.

The day Davey Hartley and his friends left for camp, McCabe and his son were up again at first light. There was just a skiff of snow on the ground as they walked to the barn to get their horses, but Mac had been right, the smell of a big storm hung heavy in the air. They'd be lucky if they got in half a day's work before it hit.

By noon huge "moon flakes" were falling and it was getting tough to see across the street. Sheriff Bob Carr waited anxiously for his son, Jerry, to show up at the office. School had been let out early and he'd told his wife the boy could stay with him and he'd bring him home later. Both of them thought that was a better idea than letting him ride his bike all the way out to the house in that storm. Besides, Jerry was a pretty good dispatcher in an emergency and his dad always gave him a few bucks if he cleaned up the place. The fact of the matter was, Jerry liked hanging around the sheriff's office just about better than any-place else.

About one-thirty in the afternoon Sheriff Carr heard Jerry's bike drop with a clatter just outside the main entrance and he smiled as his son burst through the door, slapping snow from his coat and pants.

"You think it'll snow today?" he asked jokingly.

"Naw. Just some white fungus."

Jerry hung his coat on the rack and looked around. "Doesn't look like there's much goin' on," he said, plopping down in the chair behind the dispatch radio.

"Nope," his dad replied. "I got Vernon out in the four-wheel, but I told Sid and Charley to stay home unless I needed 'em." He looked over at his son. "Looks like it's just me and you. Is that okay?"

"Hey," Jerry said, spinning around in the chair, "that's cool with me."

Their conversation was interrupted by the phone. Sheriff Carr picked it up quickly.

"This is Sheriff Carr. How can I help you?"

There was a long pause before Jerry heard his dad speak again.

"How long has he been gone?"

Jerry could see his father was scowling and he walked over and stood by his desk.

"No. Don't do anything till I get there. We'll have a bunch more of you lost in this weather."

Bob Carr hung up the phone and looked steadily at his son. "Jerry," he said softly, "there's a boy lost in this storm up at Camp Firebird. I've got to get up there. I need you to get on the radio, contact search and rescue, MedEvac, and every deputy you can raise. Can you handle it?"

"Sure, Dad!" There was not a hint of concern in his reply.

"Good! Now, the first thing I want you to do is call Sid and Charley and tell them they're on duty as of now. Sid has the other four-wheel drive, so tell him to pick up Charley and get on up to Camp Firebird. I'll get Vernon on the radio and we'll go up together. Okay! Hop to it."

Jerry popped open the phone index and started to dial a number, but before the sheriff could fire up the radio, Vernon came stomping in through the door.

"Vernon," the sheriff shouted, "just the man I was looking for." He grabbed his coat and hat off the rack, spun the startled deputy around, and pushed him toward the door before he even had a chance to wipe the snowflakes from his eyebrows.

"What . . ." he sputtered.

"I'll tell you on the way." He turned back to Jerry. "Get on it, son." The door slammed behind them and Jerry waited patiently for Sid to pick up the phone.

Two vans loaded with excited boys had pulled into the compound at Camp Firebird shortly before noon. The snow was already becoming heavy at the higher elevations and the boys had jumped out of the vans and dashed for the cabins. A short time later Davey Hartley discovered he had left his wallet in the van.

These young boys from Phoenix had never seen snow like this; in fact some of them had never seen snow at all. Davey was one of those. He looked out the window in the direction from which he thought they had come and couldn't see anything but white. But the van couldn't be more than a few yards away. He'd just dash over there, grab his wallet, and come right back.

"Better put your coat on," one of the boys told him.

"Hey, I'm just going across the road," Davey said as he disappeared out the door, and that was the last any of the boys had seen of him.

A short time later Mr. Moore, the camp counselor, had come in to give the boys their orientation talk, and when they told him Davey had gone to the van he turned as white as the snow outside. He had just come from the vans and he hadn't seen hide nor hair of Davey.

Davey Hartley hadn't gone ten feet before the falling snow had blocked his view of everything. But he was sure he knew the direction so he just kept running, expecting any second to see one or the other of them loom up in front of him.

Scientists say that when a person loses his horizon it takes less than thirty seconds to go into vertigo, a state of complete disorientation. Davey was heading straight out of camp and at a rapid pace. By the time he decided he needed help he was so far away from the camp, they couldn't hear his frightened shouts.

Mr. Moore and the other camp counselors had fanned out to the edges of the camp, shouting Davey's name into the wind, but they heard nothing in response and the snow was piling up so rapidly, any hope of finding footprints was quickly dashed. Finally they had called the sheriff's office. Davey had been missing for an hour and a half.

Elton McCabe and his son had everything buttoned up tight and had come indoors when they heard the news on the radio. Nine-year-old Davey Hartley of Phoenix, Arizona, had been missing for nearly three hours in the vicinity of Camp Firebird near State Mountain. A search party of over a hundred people, including the county Jeep posse, state search and rescue teams, and dozens of volunteers had failed to turn up any trace of the boy.

Mac turned on the TV and watched with growing concern as they interviewed Sheriff Carr, the camp counselors, and finally the boy's parents.

The snow was beginning to taper off a bit, the sheriff had said, and they could widen the search area, but Elton McCabe had spent many cold winter nights on the range and even with heavy winter gear he had nearly frozen to death a couple of times. Without even a coat he didn't give the boy much of a chance.

To Davey it was just a matter of putting one foot in front of the other. He was sure he'd run into one of the vans or the rec hall or one of the cabins any minute, but just as the snow had blocked his vision, cold and a growing fear had blocked any sense of distance or time.

They would learn later that Davey had covered an incredible six miles through the heavy snowstorm.

It was now getting dark and Davey gave up any hope of finding his way back.

Some five hours from the time he walked away from camp he came to an old drift fence, the closest thing he had seen to a structure since leaving the cabin. Using a loose board he found near a corner post he scraped away some of the snow near the fence. The wind drift had built up against the wire and a few old boards leaning against the fence had created a snow cave. Davey's scraping made a small entrance. Slowly he crawled inside and pulled the board over the opening.

At last he was out of the punishing wind. His flimsy shirt had been no protection at all and the sudden relief was almost warming. Davey fell into a deep and exhausted sleep, his only companions fear and the blistering, relentless cold.

He was out of the wind . . . but he was also invisible.

≈

Elton McCabe went to bed that night, profoundly troubled. It was almost as if it was his boy out there. He knew that mountain like the back of his hand, but he couldn't think of anyplace the boy might stumble onto that would give him the shelter he needed.

By noon the next day the number of searchers had grown to two hundred, Elton McCabe and his boy Junior among them. Media coverage had become national and all across the country people were holding prayer vigils for the lost boy.

They searched all day but no trace of Davey was found. To complicate matters the weather report was forecasting another new and even heavier storm that night.

The McCabes returned home, tired and heartsick. That night, as Mac went in to say good-night to his own son, he found it impossible to shake the image of Charlie Hartley, the father of little Davey, standing next to the sheriff, tears frozen to his cheeks, waiting in vain for some word of his lost boy.

In spite of himself Elton McCabe wiped tears from his own weathered cheeks and walked slowly back into the living room.

"That kid's been out in the cold twenty-eight hours now," he said to his wife. "Tonight's gonna dip down to ten, twelve degrees. He ain't never gonna make it."

"My heart goes out to him too," Ginny replied, "but there's nothing else we can do. They got all those folks out looking . . . you might as well try and get some sleep."

"I guess you're right," he said, "but I'm goin' up there again tomorrow."

Sleep didn't come easily to Elton McCabe that night, and when it did it was the heavy sleep that follows worry and exhaustion.

It was exactly three twenty-five A.M. when Mac sat straight up in bed with a startled cry. His wife, jolted out of her sleep, could only mumble, "What's wrong?"

"Ginny," he said, fully awake and staring into the darkness of the room, "I know where that boy is! I just dreamed it. Clear as day. That piece of old drift fence up along the south boundary of the government range . . . he's there. I got to go get him."

By four A.M. McCabe was tightening the cinch on his saddle. He was dressed in his cold-weather gear and he'd tied one of Junior's old coats and a couple of blankets in back of the saddle.

Ginny brought him a full thermos of hot coffee and was placing it carefully in one of the saddlebags just as Junior came out of the house, dressed, like his dad, for a cold ride.

"You're goin' after that kid, ain'tcha?"

"I am, son. I think I know where he is."

"I'm comin' with ya."

Elton McCabe put his arm around his son and gave him an approving hug. "Hurry," he said, "get saddled up."

None of the McCabes, not Elton, his wife, or his son, questioned the need for them to go out in the bitter cold at four o'clock in the morning to look for a lost boy whom Elton had seen only in a dream. It was just one of those things that had to be done.

By the time the gray light of dawn began to lay long shadows on the snow-covered landscape, Mac was getting discouraged. They had been heading toward the government range for two hours, but the storm had covered many of the landmarks he was used to and finding the corner of that drift fence he had seen in his dream was beginning to feel like a hopeless task.

Still, McCabe knew they were in the general area of the drift fence, so both of them began shouting the boy's name. The sound slid across the stillness of the cold and snow and faded away to nothing. There was no response.

Finally, in frustration, the elder McCabe stepped down from his horse, hoping that from ground level some of the landmarks would be more familiar. He knew he was in the right area, he just couldn't find the right spot.

"We should have come across that fence line by now," he said, half to himself and half to his son, "but everything's all drifted over." He looked up at Junior and asked, "Are you all right?"

"Aw, just a little cold, I guess," came the quick reply.

"Last time you're gonna listen to one of your old man's dreams, I'll bet." He stopped and looked around. "Maybe we should get you home."

The young McCabe brought his horse up short, "Hey, it's a lot colder for that kid," he said firmly. "Let's keep lookin'."

Mac felt a great surge of pride rise up in his chest. His land and his family were secure for at least one more generation, he was certain.

A sudden burst of wind whipped up a snow cloud and startled the horse Mac was holding loosely by the reins. The animal reared back and jumped sideways, then trotted off toward the trees.

"I'll get him," Junior said, and started off after the frightened mare.

"I got a half-frozen son and a freaked-out horse," the elder McCabe muttered to himself. "What in heaven's name am I doin' out here?"

Frustrated, tired, and full of doubt, McCabe pushed forward, driven —compelled—by the powerful vision of his unexpected dream.

"Davey! Davey Hartley!" he shouted, but the only thing that came back to him was the echo.

Struggling through the snow to the top of a small rise he stopped to look around. His breath caught in his throat as he saw before him the corner of the drift fence exactly as he had seen it in his dream. Instantly he was fully energized and he drove forward through the deep snow with powerful strides. The boy was there. He had to be there.

By the time Junior rode up with the runaway horse Mac had dug away the rude shelter and was lifting the boy's still form from its hiding place. He was pale and his skin felt like ice, but a slight flicker of his eyelids told McCabe that he was, miraculously, still alive.

"The coat, son, and those blankets, get them for me. Hurry!"

Junior slid from his horse without hesitation and in moments Davey Hartley was wrapped and bundled and held tightly to the chest of the elder McCabe as he climbed aboard his horse and turned back toward the ranch house. Junior rode alongside, urging the animals forward as fast as the deep drifts would allow.

It would be touch and go for a while, but Davey Hartley finally came back to the land of the living. He would tell his parents that he had heard someone calling his name, just as in his dream, and the first thing he remembered seeing was a man on a horse.

It was several weeks before Elton McCabe and Davey Hartley had a chance to talk to each other. The subject of their respective dreams came up only by chance. They both knew, however, that something far greater than chance had been at work in their lives.

Dave Hartley is now in his mid-twenties. He doesn't talk much about his experience, unless someone asks. I found it interesting that he really didn't make a big thing out of what, to most people, was a miraculous event. It happened and he is alive today because it happened.

Nothing in rational thought can explain either his dream or the startling vision that interrupted Elton McCabe's sleep. As far as Davey is concerned that's just the way things are.

Dave Hartley did take one thing off that mountain, however: the seeds of the McCabe family's willingness to help a neighbor. He brought those seeds home and planted them in his own neighborhood. Now, he says, everyone helps his neighbor every chance he gets.

And Ginny McCabe finds her husband sitting next to her in the pew at Sunday services just about every week now. She says it's been like that for the past fifteen years. But that's the way miracles are—they have very far-reaching effects, much farther than we realize.

Maybe that's the reason they happen so often.

CHAPTER 4

THE LADY IN THE SNOW

≈≈≈

BEALS, WYOMING, POPULATION 2,501. MANY CITY PEOPLE DREAM OF A place like this. Clean, clear air, elbow room, the wide-open spaces. God's country, some call it. But Will Anders wasn't thinking about any of that when he decided to move back here.

Will's two children, Cassie, age thirteen, and Abel, age seven, had both been born and spent most of their lives in the Bay Area near San Francisco. Will was a successful computer installation specialist and business was good. He and his wife, Christine, had planned on making their home there forever.

Christine had been a vital and loving mother. The kind of mother that ran and laughed in the sun with her children, never suspecting that the malignancy growing inside her would take her life without warning.

What was left behind was a young father, a little girl just into her teens, a bewildered little boy, and a very large and aching void in their lives.

Will watched with growing consternation as grief invaded his home and began to take its toll on himself and his children. After struggling mightily with all the pros and cons he decided that what was needed were new surroundings, new friends, and a fresh look at life. His experience as a computer technician brought him many offers from all over the country, but in the final analysis he decided to just go back to his boyhood home in Wyoming. Even though his parents were both gone, there was still a support system there and a sense of belonging. Instinctively he knew he needed that.

The Anders family had settled in quickly in Will's old hometown. They found a house on the edge of town but close enough to the school and the grocery store that Abel and Cassie could walk to most places they needed to be.

Cassie was a serious girl, slight of build and as energetic as any thirteen-year-old, but Will had some concerns. She was, he thought, shedding her childhood much too quickly in an effort to take her mother's place in the family. Will sensed all of this, but he didn't know what he could do about it and as he looked over the neatly laid-out dinner, the result of Cassie's efforts, the only thing that seemed appropriate was a compliment.

"Looks great and smells great, Cassie," he said as they all took their places at the table.

"Just the same old stuff," Cassie replied.

"Well, I guess maybe we like the same old stuff, right, Abel?" Will tousled his son's hair and added, "Why don't you say the blessing for us?"

Without hesitation Abel folded his arms and bowed his head: "Come, Lord Jesus, be our guest, and let this food to us be blessed. Amen."

Will smiled and handed Abel the bowl of potatoes. It was a tradition in their house that whoever blessed the food got the first serving.

"George Burke got some new videos," Abel said, helping himself to the biggest potato in the bowl. "Can I go over to his house tomorrow after school on the bus? His mom already said okay."

"I guess so," Will replied. "I'll pick you up there on my way home." He looked over at Cassie and asked, "How about you, sweetheart? You got anything planned for after school?"

"No, not really." She paused. "Well, Mrs. Larkin called. She has rheumatism and asked me if I could stop at the pharmacy and pick her up a few things."

Will frowned in spite of himself. He was proud that Mrs. Larkin and the other ladies in the neighborhood had come to realize that Cassie was willing to help them out when she could, but he was still concerned that she was losing her childhood.

Setting up a new business in a small town was time consuming, and Will was already feeling a little bit guilty with the fact that he relied on Cassie too much himself. She took care of Abel, the house, and the meals and did the shopping. And somehow she found time to help out around the neighborhood. He knew the only way she could do that was by giving up all her school activities and friends.

"Cassie"—his tone was serious—"I think it's really great that you're so willing to help out, but isn't there something you'd like to be doing at school? Some friends . . . ?"

"No, Daddy!" Her answer was firm and matter-of-fact.

"Okay, but I want you to know, if there's something you need to do in school or want to do with your friends we can always get someone to come in and—"

"Why? Don't I do a good job?"

Will was walking on thin ice again and he knew it. Once again she had put him in a no-win position. No matter which way he answered her question it would be wrong. As usual he took the easy way out.

"You do a great job," he said, leaning over and kissing her on the forehead, "and I'm very proud of you."

"We all have to be strong," Cassie said without looking up from her meal.

Will knew that he was looking at a little girl with amazing strength of character. She had seen the need to fill her mother's shoes and that was what she was doing.

Ah, well, he thought, *maybe it's better this way.*

If Will had followed Cassie into her room that night he might have had second thoughts. Alone in the silence of her room, Cassie reached over and took her mother's picture from the nightstand and held it tightly to her breast. A moment later she laid her head on her pillow and quietly cried herself to sleep.

By the time Will and Abel came into the kitchen the next morning Cassie had breakfast on the table and lunches, all neatly packed, were on the kitchen counter.

"Hi, honey," Will said brightly, sitting down at the table. "Where's your little brother?"

"Probably in the other room with his nose in a comic book," she replied.

Will poured himself a cup of coffee and switched on the radio. "Abel . . . breakfast. You can help Superman save the world later."

Abel came through the kitchen door and slid into his usual chair at the table. There was a glass of orange juice in front of him and fresh toast on his plate. Cassie was nothing if not efficient.

They were just finishing up when the announcer on the radio said something that got Will's attention:

"Well, folks, that cold system that's been rumbling around the Kenai Peninsula in Alaska finally got its act together. The first 'Siberian Express' of the season could be headed our way. Right now a massive cold front is howling across Alaska and forecasters say it could make a sharp right turn around the Canadian Yukon and roar right straight down through 'iceberg alley,' into our backyard. So if you've been enjoying this tropical fall weather, with temperatures in the fifties, now's the time to pack away your bikinis and suntan oil and pull out the old sheepskin coat, earmuffs, and leather mittens. This could be a cold one.''

Will had been listening carefully to every word. Like most Wyoming natives he could describe the effects of the phenomenon called the "Siberian Express" in numbing detail. These mammoth cold fronts could roar down out of Canada with alarming speed, sometimes without any warning, and they had been known to drop temperatures as much as fifty degrees in less than an hour. A warning that one might be on the way was not to be taken lightly.

"Did you kids hear that?" he asked.

Neither of them had paid any attention. After all, there weren't any pictures on the radio.

"I want both of you to take your heavy coats today. Not your jacket, your coat. Understand?"

Cassie was busily cleaning up the kitchen. She looked out the window at the bright sunshine that was beginning to scare away the frost on Mrs. Larkin's pasture in back of their house. *I'll just have to lug that big heavy thing around with me all day,* she thought, but she nodded her understanding anyway.

Will looked over at Abel, who nodded also. "Good," he said. "Now, don't forget."

Their father disappeared into the next room and returned packing his own heavy winter coat. "Abel," he said, gathering up his briefcase, "I'm already running a little late, so I might not pick you up as early as I thought. You stay at the Burkes' until I come for you, all right?"

"Yeah!"

"A little more disappointment would be appreciated," Will said with a smile, then turned to Cassie. "You come right home after school," he said.

"Well, I have to pick up those things for Mrs. Larkin."

"That means you'll miss the bus," Will said with obvious concern.

"It's not like it's that far," she replied. "Sometimes I walk just for the fun of it."

Will thought about it for a moment. She was right, it wasn't really that far and if she took her winter coat she should be fine.

"Okay," he said finally, "but don't dawdle."

As Will climbed into his station wagon cluttered with spare computer parts and instruction manuals, he was strangely uneasy. He started the car, then almost got back out to go tell Cassie to forget Mrs. Larkin's medicine and come home on the bus; but he talked himself out of it. What would he say to Mrs. Larkin?

Cassie finished putting the dishes in the dishwasher, handed Abel his lunch, picked up her own, and started for the door.

"Dad said to wear your winter coat?" Abel reminded her as he struggled to get into his own hooded parka.

"I know," she said, "but I'll be home early." She grabbed the light jacket she'd been wearing to school from the peg by the door. "Hurry," she said, pushing him out the door, "we'll miss the bus."

The uneasiness Will felt when he left the house that morning stayed with him all day. Lacking any other explanation he put it down to the change in the weather he felt was coming, even though by the time he took a break for lunch the sun was still shining brightly and the temperature was in the high forties.

Shortly after lunch Herb, a young technician Will had hired to work part-time, showed up to begin checking out a new shipment of circuit boards. He came through the door carrying a three-quarter length sheepskin coat and a hat to match and hung them both on the rack by the door.

"Looks like you heard the weather forecast too," Will said. "You think that Siberian Express has finally kicked loose?"

"I don't know," Herb replied, "but I'm not takin' any chances. My daddy taught me a long time ago," he added, jerking his thumb toward the coat rack, "you can always hang it on the rack if you don't need it, but if you need it and you ain't got it, there's no way to put it on."

Will nodded and smiled, but Herb's comment sharply accentuated the uneasy feelings he had been struggling with all morning. "Okay, Herb," he said, trying to shake it off, "what d'ya say we get to work on these circuit boards? We got two packages of five each this morning. With a little luck I can have them all in place by the end of the day."

When Will had purchased the ranch house on the outskirts of town he had done so seeking the semiisolation and extra property this particular place afforded. Most kids in this part of the world learned very early on to take care of themselves. It was, Will felt, being out away from everyone else that contributed to the kind of independence and self-esteem he wanted for Cassie and Abel. So far as he could tell, they were pleased with the arrangement.

In actuality they were only about a mile and a half from town. Their nearest neighbor, the Larkins, were maybe a half mile down the road. The Larkins were an older couple with no children. Ed Larkin drove a logging truck most of the time and was frequently gone for days or even weeks at a time. His wife, May, called on Cassie frequently, as much for the company as anything, Will thought.

Their house was set well back on a plot of land that was about ten acres in size. Ed had farmed it, alfalfa mostly, when he was a younger man, but now most of it was parceled off into pasture that Mr. Larkin rented out in the summertime. The Larkins' property line on the north side was the fence between one of these pastures and Will's acre and a half.

Cassie, in addition to her other chores, had taken the responsibility of doing the marketing. She had a cloth bag she took with her to school on the days she needed something at the store. After school she would pick up the things she needed and simply walk home. She did this fairly frequently except when the weather got really bad; then she would wait until Saturday so Will could take her to the store.

Once, during one of these walks, she had discovered a cattle gate in the Larkins' fence. It didn't take her long to figure out that by going across the pasture to her backyard she could shorten her walk by nearly a half mile. She had taken this shortcut many times and had even found the easiest ways to get around or under or through the other fences that divided the property.

Cassie got out of school around three P.M. and realized the weather had turned a little crisp. Still, it didn't seem too bad, and she had picked up Mrs. Larkin's medicine and was on her way home by three-thirty.

By the time she got to the cattle gate she had buttoned the light jacket clear to her chin, but the increasing velocity of the wind was still biting right through it. She looked across the fields and realized that going to the Larkins' house first would make it less of a shortcut, but the sooner she could get out of that wind the better. Cassie unsnapped the chain that held the gate closed, stepped through it, then carefully put the chain back in place and started across the field at a brisk pace.

Unless you've been caught in one it's hard to imagine the awesome and violent power of the "Siberian Express." At first there's just a little increase in the wind and a sudden drop in temperature. Within half an hour the sky turns dark as great black clouds roll down from the north, and old-timers will tell you the wind that brings them can make a logging chain stand straight out.

Cassie had her head down and her chin tucked in against the ever-increasing blasts of cold wind. The cloth bag with Mrs. Larkin's pills was clutched tightly in one hand as she tried to pick up the pace and run.

Maybe if she hadn't had her head down, maybe if she hadn't been trying to run, she would have seen the gopher hole. But she didn't. In a split second her foot jammed into the opening and she went down. She felt the pain and heard the bone in her leg snap almost simultaneously.

In that instant everything in her young life changed. A few moments before she had just been uncomfortable with a warm house just a few hundred yards away. Now, as she cried out in pain, she realized that she was totally, completely, alone and helpless. Even without the wind, whose awful howl was now turning into a violent scream, she was not close enough to either house to be heard.

Will looked up from his workbench and shuddered at the fury of the storm. This would be a beaut. He looked at his watch. The time was only four-thirty and already it was like night outside. The wind rattled the windows in his office as he stared out into the already deserted street. The strange sense of foreboding he had experienced earlier in the day crept back into his heart.

"Are you worrying about these serial ports?" Herb asked.

The question brought him back to the task at hand. "No, they'll be all right. I'm just . . . I don't know, I've had this strange feeling all day, like something was wrong."

"I've got a strange feeling too," Herb replied, "and it's telling me we aren't going to get this thing wrapped up tonight."

"Yeah," Will said, "you're right. Let's call it a day."

Herb slipped into the sheepskin coat and hat he had carried in earlier, gave Will a thumbs-up, and braced himself for the blast he knew he was going to get on the other side of the door. As he left Will shuddered involuntarily once again at the sound of the wind screaming down across the valley.

Will Anders tossed a few things in his briefcase and snapped it closed, then slipped on his own heavy winter coat and started for the door. At the last minute he remembered some invoices he was going to check and quickly grabbed them from the top of the desk. As he turned out the lights he was struck again by the depth of the darkness so early in the day.

It was now nearly an hour since Cassie had opened up the pasture gate and started for the Larkins' home. The temperature was already below the freezing mark, and even though she tried to drag herself toward the house, the intense pain soon sapped what little strength she had.

Cassie knew the gravity of her situation and she knew that if she didn't get help soon she would surely die. But it wasn't the fear of death that brought the greatest sorrow to her heart, it was the thought of what her death would do to her father and brother so soon after the loss of their mother. Shivering in a blinding cold, racked with pain and unable to move, little Cassie Anders could only think of the grief her father would have to bear if she didn't survive.

Will made a dash for his car, tossed the briefcase inside, and laid the invoices carefully on top. Now as he made his way toward the Burkes' to pick up Abel he found himself gripping the steering wheel tightly against the buffeting of the fierce winds.

As he turned a corner Will reached out instinctively to hold the invoices in place, but he couldn't feel them. He looked down briefly but couldn't see them either. Angrily he pulled the car to a stop and checked all around the seat and floorboards. They weren't there. He must have grabbed something else by mistake.

With a jerk Will turned the car around and headed back to the office. How could he have made such a stupid mistake?

For nearly two hours Cassie had been lying in the open field. Except for her broken leg, which protruded piteously, she had rolled herself up into a tight little ball to try and protect herself against the cold, but there was nothing she could do to stave off the rampaging wind and numbing cold that came with it.

Relentlessly the wind ripped at her as the temperature continued to fall, now well below freezing, and she could feel the warmth of life beginning to slip away. It was cold, so very cold. Maybe if she could just go to sleep for a little while.

Little Cassie Anders was about to give up and drift away when she heard a voice calling her name. It was a soft voice, gentle, like her mother's, and it came sharply to her ears in spite of the roar of the wind.

Cassie opened her eyes, searching the darkness. At last she could make out a form. It was a woman, much older than her mother, but full of kindness, she could tell. The woman carried a heavy winter coat and quickly knelt next to Cassie, slipped the coat around her shivering shoulders, and tucked it up tight under her chin.

"Who are you?" Cassie asked, through chattering teeth. "How did you find me?" The words had trouble getting past her lips, but the coat and the warmth of the woman's embrace had given Cassie new hope.

"I heard you crying, dear," the woman said, "and I came because I'm not going to let a freezing cold night carry you off."

Cassie turned inside the coat and pulled her uninjured leg up as far as she could to take advantage of the warmth. In the process one of the buttons on the coat came loose in her hand and she clutched it tightly.

"Now, don't you worry," the woman said soothingly, "your father will be here soon."

Cassie didn't know how that could be, but then she didn't know how this woman had found her either. She just moved in as close as she could to the woman's warm embrace and waited.

Will pulled up to the front door of his office and bolted from the car. It took him a minute or two to get the key in the lock but finally the door swung open and he flicked on the light. He went straight to the desk and began to push papers aside looking for the invoices. He was still looking when the phone rang.

At first he thought of just letting it ring. He wasn't about to solve anyone's computer problems the rest of this day, but even as the thought crossed his mind he lifted the phone from its cradle.

"This is Will Anders," he said flatly.

"Mr. Anders"—it was a woman's voice, soft and unflustered—"my name is Lillian Morgan. Mr. Anders, you must hurry if you are going to save your dear little Cassie. She has fallen in the back pasture and broken her leg. She is in danger of freezing to death, Mr. Anders. You must hurry."

Will was too stunned to respond. He stared at the telephone. Surely this was a joke. Yet somewhere deep inside he knew it wasn't. He dropped the phone and raced to his car. The back pasture. Even as he turned the station wagon around he was remembering Cassie telling him about her shortcut across the pasture. She had even pointed out the gate one day as they drove by. That must be what the woman meant.

With an urgency in his chest that he had never felt before, Will Anders pushed the vehicle through the storm. *Cassie, oh, Cassie,* he thought, *please, please hang on.*

Cassie turned to look up into the woman's face. She was smiling and Cassie thought she could hear her humming.

"Are you sure my daddy is coming?" she asked.

"Oh, yes, he surely is." The woman put both arms around Cassie's shoulders and whispered, "You can close your eyes now, darling. I'll watch over you till your daddy comes."

Suddenly the headlights of Will's station wagon illuminated the pasture. Cassie tried to sit up but she didn't have the strength.

Will looked out into the beam of his lights and rubbed his eyes. Someone was definitely there.

"Cassie!" he screamed against the wind.

Quickly he threw open the gate and raced across the frozen pasture toward the figure he could see only dimly in his headlights.

"Cassie, is that you?" he cried out again.

Cassie was trying to answer back but no sound would come.

"Don't worry, little one," the woman said, "your daddy has found you."

In the next instant Will Anders was standing over the huddled and broken body of his daughter.

"Oh, Cassie." He sobbed and lifted her up in his strong arms. The heavy wool coat that had been tucked around her was gone and Will quickly wrapped her up in his own heavy coat. Her leg was broken, the woman had said on the phone, he must get her to a doctor.

"Oh, Daddy, you found me," Cassie said, the words barely audible in the roar of the wind, "just like the lady said you would."

"What lady, sweetheart?" Will was laying her down gently on the backseat of the station wagon.

"The one who put the coat around me." Cassie sat up and tried to look, but she didn't have enough strength.

"She was just here, Daddy, she told me you were coming."

Too many things were happening too fast for Will Anders. He would take up the story of the woman later. Right now he had to get Cassie to the doctor.

But Will had one more surprise in store. As he opened the door to slip in under the steering wheel the dome light came on. There, neatly stacked on top of his briefcase, were the invoices he had gone back to the office to find.

Will slammed the car into reverse, spun around, and headed straight for the small medical clinic that served as doctor's office, emergency room, and hospital. Driving through the storm he could feel the power of it slam into his vehicle. He glanced down at the invoices. *What if I hadn't gone back for them?* he wondered. *What if I hadn't been there to take that phone call?*

They kept Cassie at the clinic for a couple of days, just to make sure she wasn't suffering any aftereffects of the hypothermia. The doctor told Will he couldn't understand how she had survived. Even a grown man, out in that kind of cold with no coat and a broken leg, should have been dead.

Cassie told them about the lady and about the old wool coat she had put around her, but the doctor, and Will, too, if the truth were known, just chalked it up to delirium. Of course Will had thought he had seen someone in the headlights, kneeling next to Cassie, but there hadn't been anyone there, and there was certainly no coat.

But what of the phone call?

When they got home, Cassie told her father the story once again. How the lady had come to her just as she was beginning to give up, and how she had wrapped her in this warm wool coat and told her that her own little girl had died in a storm like that. And this time she handed Will the curious old button from the coat that had come off in her hand.

"We have to find her, Daddy," she said with conviction, "we just have to. We have to thank her."

Will turned the button over and over in his hand. He hadn't seen anything like it since he was a kid, but he recognized it as the kind of leather button used on wool coats way back when. His mother had owned a coat with buttons almost like this one.

"Okay," Will said, "a woman named Lillian Morgan called and told me where to find you. We'll see if we can find her and go from there. If nothing else I owe her a great big thank-you too."

Will and Cassie spent the next couple of days scouring the phone books of Jackson County. Finally they found a Lillian Morgan listed over in Twin Buttes. Will loaded Cassie and Abel into the station wagon and off they went. An hour later they were ringing the doorbell on one of the older homes in town. A woman in her mid-sixties came to the door.

"Miss Lillian Morgan?" Will asked hopefully.

"No," the woman replied, "that's my sister. Might I ask why you want to see her?"

Will retold the story carefully, with special emphasis on the phone call and the fact that the woman had told him her name was Lillian Morgan.

The woman who greeted them identified herself as Mrs. Holt. She listened attentively but when Will had finished she simply shook her head.

"I believe you, Mr. Anders," she said, "but I'm afraid it couldn't be my sister. It must have been another Lillian Morgan."

"You're sure?" Cassie was crestfallen. "Are you absolutely positive?"

Mrs. Holt looked into the sad, hopeful eyes of the young girl with a cast on her leg and motioned for them to follow her.

"Please be very quiet," she said.

Mrs. Holt led Will and Cassie and Abel down a narrow hallway to a back room. Carefully she opened the door and peered inside, then invited them to come in with her.

There, in a wheelchair, next to the window, sat Lillian Morgan. She didn't seem even to notice when they came into the room. But Cassie's eyes brightened as soon as she saw her and she turned excitedly to her father.

"That's her, Daddy, the lady that came and put the coat over me. She talked to me and kept me warm."

Mrs. Holt looked up at Will and shook her head sadly, "I'm sorry," she said, "that's quite impossible. My sister has been totally paralyzed for the past six years. She can't even speak."

"When I found her," Will said, offering Mrs. Holt the button, "Cassie had this clasped in her hand. Does it mean anything to you?"

Mrs. Holt gasped and hurried off into another room as Cassie made her way around to the front of the wheelchair.

"You saved me, didn't you?" she said, throwing her arms around Lillian Morgan. "I don't know how but you did it."

Cassie was still standing next to Mrs. Morgan when Mrs. Holt returned with a heavy winter coat over her arm. There was a button missing, and the one Cassie had held on to so tightly that night matched the others perfectly.

"This coat belonged to her daughter," Mrs. Holt told them. "Her name was Margaret." She paused as the memory caught in her throat, but finally she said to Cassie, "Margaret was just about your age when she got caught in a blizzard and froze to death. But that was a long, long time ago."

There may have still been some doubts in the mind of Mrs. Holt but there was none in Cassie's mind. She leaned forward and kissed Lillian Morgan on the cheek.

"Thank you," she said softly, "thank you very much."

As the Anders family turned to go, Mrs. Holt couldn't help noticing a single tear drifting down the cheek of her sister.

On the way home in the station wagon Cassie turned to her father and said, "I don't know why, Daddy, but all that's happened has made me think more of Momma. Not in a sad way, but in a way that helps me understand more about people. I mean, we're all connected, aren't we, Daddy?"

Will Anders put his arm around his daughter and gave her a hug.

"Yes," he said, "we are."

Sitting around the house with her leg in a cast, Cassie had a lot of time to think about what had happened to her, and she decided that if

Lillian Morgan could hear her crying in a storm like that, and somehow come to her and speak to her when she hadn't been able to move or speak to anyone else in years, then maybe her mother wasn't very far away either. She liked to think that maybe her mother and Lillian Morgan's daughter had somehow helped Lillian find her in that bleak and freezing pasture.

Cassie grew up to be a beautiful young woman, active in school and community affairs. She visited Lillian Morgan regularly right up to the day Mrs. Morgan died. Lillian Morgan never spoke to her again, except, as Cassie said, heart to heart. But they had shared something special, something miraculous, and they both knew it.

Cassie doesn't spend a lot of time trying to figure out how it happened, or even why, but she has never forgotten that it was nothing less than a miracle that saved her life.

As far as the rest of the Anders family of Jackson County, Wyoming, is concerned, no explanation is necessary; they simply accept it and cherish it in their hearts.

CHAPTER 5

ANGELS AT
THE ROADSIDE

≈≈≈

IN TODAY'S WORLD MOST OF US THINK NOTHING OF CLIMBING IN THE CAR AND driving across the state or even across the country. Millions of miles of paved roads crisscrossing the nation, and automobiles that offer literally all the comforts of home, make it a foregone conclusion that you can get just about anywhere you want to go in comparative comfort and ease.

It was in this unconcerned frame of mind that Harry Linden and his wife, Ruth, made plans for their move to Arizona.

Harry Linden was in the army. His reassignment made the move necessary, and in typical army fashion he was required to go with his unit on twenty-four-hour notice. That meant that Ruth and their four-year-old daughter, Becky, would have to be responsible for getting themselves and their household goods to their new home.

This wasn't exactly a new experience for the Lindens, and as always they simply tried to make the best of it. In this particular instance making the best of it included an opportunity for Ruth to make a stopover in Santa Rosa, New Mexico, and spend a little time with her sister, Lucy, whom she hadn't seen in years. From that standpoint, at least, both Ruth and Becky were looking forward to the trip.

The day the movers came to load up the furniture Ruth gave Becky a box of crayons and some paper and told her to stay in the kitchen and draw. That suited Becky just fine. Ruth commandeered a small end table for her to use and she began creating her masterpiece.

Everything went smoothly. Army families learn quickly that it doesn't pay to have too many possessions when the head of the family is a young officer subject to sudden long-distance moves. A breakfast set, bedroom set, refrigerator, couch, Harry's favorite chair—and the TV, of course—plus a few boxes of personal things, clothes, dishes, pans, those sorts of things, were all that needed to be loaded up.

The movers were down to the small end table Becky was using as a drawing board when Ruth came into the now empty room to tell her they were ready to go.

"I'm ready, too, Mommy," Becky said, proudly showing her mother the picture she'd been working on. It was a man and a woman standing side by side. The man looked as if he might be wearing overalls and a straw hat. The woman was holding his hand.

"Hey, that's very good, Becky," Ruth said. "Is it somebody we know?"

"Nope," Becky replied, "just some nice people in New Mexico."

Ruth smiled and gave the piece of paper back to her daughter. Then she noticed Becky was still clinging to one of her favorite toys, a small music box with an angel, which looked to be about Becky's age, standing on top.

"Oh, honey," Ruth said, "I thought you were going to put that in the box with your other toys."

"Can't I take it with me in the car, Mommy, there's plenty of room, please?"

Ruth hesitated for a moment, then decided it was more important that her daughter learn early on that it was important to stick with the plan.

"Now, Becky," her mother said, kneeling beside her, "you know we talked about this. Look." She took the toy from her daughter's hand. "One hand is already broken. What if one of the wings were to get broken, bouncing around in the car? You wouldn't want that to happen, would you?"

Becky looked down at the floor and stuck out her lower lip. "No," she said sadly, then added, "But she's my favorite, she looks after me."

"All right." Ruth stood up. "I'll pack it right in the top of your toy box so you can get to it first thing when we get to our new home."

That seemed to help. Becky took her mother's hand and they walked out the door. One of the moving men brought the small end table; the other picked up Ruth and Becky's suitcases and took them to the car.

Becky waited patiently in the front seat while her mother packed away the angel music box and made sure the suitcases were properly stored in the trunk. At last Ruth climbed into the driver's seat, took one last look at what had been their home for the past couple of years, and started the car.

"Here we go," Ruth said. "Next stop, Aunt Lucy's."

Becky strained to look out the windshield as they backed out of the driveway. She would miss her swing in the backyard and her friends, but it would be fun to see Aunt Lucy again.

"Did you bring my medicine, Mommy?"

"Sure did." Ruth patted the bag she had placed between them on the front seat. "It's right in here. But you're not going to get sick this time, okay?"

"Okay," Becky replied without much conviction. Then she settled back in the seat and began to put some finishing touches on the picture she had drawn.

Ruth glanced at it once again out of the corner of her eye. *That's really quite good for a four-year-old,* she thought. And it was a comforting feeling to know that her daughter had the right kind of expectations.

They had put nearly four hundred miles behind them by the time they pulled into the driveway of Lucy's home in Santa Rosa. Becky had been asleep for the last hour or so, but she woke up when the car pulled to a stop and she heard her aunt Lucy come flying out the front door.

"Oh, Ruth," she cried, enclosing her in a huge bear hug, "you've made such good time." Then, without waiting for a response, Lucy released her sister and pulled open the passenger door of the car. "Oh, and, Becky, it's so good to see you again." She reached down and scooped her up, almost taking her breath away, she squeezed her so hard. "I can't believe how you've grown. Come in, come in."

Once inside her sister's comfortable home Ruth had a chance to relax. Eight hours on the road at one stretch was a little more than she liked to do, but she had really wanted to get here the first day. Maybe she'd take it in smaller steps the rest of the way, but for now everything was just fine. It had been worth it.

"Oh," Lucy said, "I almost forgot. Harry called a little while ago and left a number where you can reach him. He wanted me to have you call the minute you got here."

"Fantastic," Ruth said, rising quickly from her comfortable spot on the couch. "Becky, come on, we're going to talk to Daddy."

Becky jumped down from Aunt Lucy's lap and followed her mother into the kitchen, where the phone was located.

"That's the number right there on that yellow pad," Lucy called to them, "the one with the 602 area code."

Another of the miracles of our modern life soon brought Harry and Ruth together.

"I hate it," Harry told her, "when you get stuck with all the packing."

"There really isn't that much to it," Ruth replied. "I just hate it when we can't make the move together."

"Yeah, me too," Harry said. "If they'd given us a few more days' notice we could have worked it out, but that's army intelligence for you."

"Excuse me," Ruth said with a laugh, "but isn't that a contradiction in terms?"

She heard Harry laugh on the other end of the line, and then he asked to speak to Becky.

"Hi, Daddy. Are you there already?"

"Yep, I sure am, and I can hardly wait for you to get here. How's my girl so far?"

"I'm okay, Daddy. My stomach just hurts a little bit."

Ruth frowned when she heard that. Becky hadn't complained the whole trip, and she had decided maybe her daughter had outgrown her "travel pains."

Becky handed the phone back to her mother and ran back to Aunt Lucy's comfortable lap.

"She didn't say anything to me all day," Ruth told her husband, "but I'll give her some of that stuff the doctor told me to use for her stomachache. We'll be all right."

"I love you, babe," Harry whispered into her ear. "Drive carefully, but get here as soon as you can."

"I love you too." Ruth sighed. "Look for us day after tomorrow."

"It's a deal. Give Becky a kiss for me."

"Sure thing."

Ruth held the phone to her ear until she heard the dial tone and wondered why it was always so much harder to say good-bye on the phone than in person. Ah, well, just two more days. She could handle it.

When she walked back into the living room Ruth noticed that Becky was all curled up in a little knot on her aunt Lucy's lap.

"You didn't tell me you had a tummyache," Ruth said, reaching down and picking her up.

"Well, it's not a very bad one," Becky responded.

"Okay, but let's fix it anyway."

Ruth handed her back to Lucy and went out to the car to get the medicine from her bag. She was not overly concerned. For some reason Becky almost always got a stomachache riding in the car. This had been an extra-long ride and she had held up very well. The doctor had told her he thought it was mostly anxiety anyway and Becky would probably grow out of it. When she didn't complain all day Ruth had dared to think that maybe she was doing just that.

The interior lights of the car went on as Ruth opened the door, and she reached in and grabbed the bag. No sense in rummaging through it in the dim light of the car. As she pulled it toward her, she felt, more than saw, something fall against the seat. When she looked closer she saw that it was Becky's little music box with the dancing angel on top. It must have been leaning against the bag.

"How in the world . . ." Ruth muttered, as she picked up the toy to look at it more closely. "I'm sure I packed that away."

Maybe the mover felt sorry for her and sneaked it back while I wasn't looking, she thought, but even as she turned the idea over in her mind she knew it couldn't have happened that way. Well, it wasn't a big deal and now that it was here it might help Becky feel better. She slipped it into the bag and went back in the house.

Lucy carried Becky back into the kitchen and sat her on the counter-top as Ruth fished the bottle of antacid from the bag and measured out a spoonful.

"Here you go," she said, slipping the spoon into Becky's mouth.

Becky took it bravely and swallowed, then grimaced involuntarily and stuck out her tongue as the full impact of the stuff hit her taste buds.

"I wish I didn't get stomachaches," she said.

"I wish you didn't either," her mother replied, "but this will help make it better."

Ruth reached into the bag and produced the little angel music box. Becky's reaction was explosive delight.

"Oh, thank you, Mommy, thank you," she squealed, hugging the poor, dilapidated little toy to her chest. "I know I'll be better now."

The puzzle of how it had gotten there was quickly forgotten in the sheer pleasure of her daughter's happiness.

Ruth and Becky were up early the next morning, anxious to be on the road again. Lucy tried to persuade her to spend an extra day with her but all to no avail. She had promised Harry she'd be there sometime the following day, and as far as she was concerned the earlier the better.

Becky climbed into the front seat and waited patiently for Aunt Lucy to buckle the seat belt and give her another dozen kisses. Then she carefully placed the music box on top of her picture and announced she was ready to go.

"Well, I guess that's it, then." Ruth laughed. "We'd better be on our way."

There was one more round of hugs and a quick check of the road map and they were off. Going over the map with Lucy the night before, Ruth had decided to take Highway 54 south and cut across to I-10 that way, leaving her a straight freeway shot for the rest of the trip.

Lucy tried to explain that I-40 West and then South down I-25 until it turned into I-10 was a much better road and would probably make for a much more comfortable drive, but Becky's stomach problem seemed to be gone and the Highway 54 option would save two, maybe three hours.

The trip for the first hour or so was uneventful. Ruth stopped at Vaughn and gassed up, and gave Becky a chance to go to the bathroom and walk around a bit. She seemed to be doing just fine. As she got back in under the steering wheel, Ruth felt good about her decision to take the shorter route.

Highway 54 is one of the standard two-lane highways that crosses much of western America. At one time these were the routes that took everyone to and from the various towns and cities, but since the advent of the interstate system they were only lightly traveled and not terribly well maintained.

With the early start Ruth was making good time, but not long after they left Vaughn Becky had begun to complain about her stomach again. Ruth stopped long enough to give her another spoonful of medicine and make sure that she could get at her paper and crayons. Maybe, she thought, if she could get her mind off the road, the stomachache would go away.

It had worked, but only temporarily, and as Becky's pain seemed to intensify Ruth began looking for road signs that would indicate the presence of a town, any town, that might be big enough to have a doctor. On Highway 54 they were few and far between.

At last Ruth spotted a sign. CEDARVALE 28 was all that it said, and an arrow pointed to a side road off to her left that looked for all the world as if it was going no place except deeper into the desert.

Becky's complaining had now turned into an almost constant whimper. Ruth could tell that she was trying to be a big girl and not cry, but it was becoming more and more difficult for her. Ruth took the left-hand turn at the junction and pointed the car toward Cedarvale.

"It's all right, Becky," she said soothingly, "we'll stop in this town up here in just a few minutes and see if we can't make it all better."

Becky's only response was to try and cuddle up into a little ball. Ruth looked over at her and noticed little beads of sweat had begun to form around her hairline, and for the first time she regretted not having taken the more traveled route. It had not escaped her notice that she hadn't passed another vehicle going in either direction since she'd turned onto the road to Cedarvale.

The desert drifted away on either side of the road and she could see nothing but a line of low, rolling hills up ahead. Suddenly a loud screech and a banging sound exploded from under her hood. Before she could get the car fully stopped, the temperature light had blinked on and steam was pouring out from under the hood.

The first prickly sensations of fear began to creep over her as she looked over at Becky.

"What happened to the car, Mommy?"

"I don't know, honey," was the honest reply. "Maybe it's nothing bad." That last part didn't feel terribly honest. The fact was it had sounded to her as if the whole engine had blown up.

She turned it off, got out of the car, carefully opened the hood, and looked inside. She was not unfamiliar with engines, but she was no mechanic either; if it was anything very serious she would be in big trouble. A quick glance confirmed the worst. The pulley on the fan had come apart, leaving the fan belt that turned the water pump practically useless.

Frustrated, angry with herself for having put them in such a vulnerable position, and with a growing fear about her daughter's illness, Ruth could do nothing except stare up and down the lonely road and hope that someone would soon come by. Someone who would be willing to stop and help them.

At first she thought it would be best if she stood by the car, ready to flag down any passing motorist, but when Becky began to cry she quickly got back inside. By keeping a close eye on the rearview mirror as well as watching out the front she should be able to spot any oncoming vehicles in time to jump out and flag them down.

Becky was now in a lot of pain. As Ruth pulled her closer she could feel the fever in her brow, and the fear turned to a thick lump in her throat. Whatever was going on, it was not something an antacid could fix.

Anxiously Ruth scanned the road in both directions. Nothing moved and she wasn't even sure how far she was from Cedarvale, or anywhere else for that matter. Looking over the barren landscape she thought she might as well be on the moon.

Becky had been clinging to her favorite toy but now she let it fall. Ruth reached down, picked it up, and for some unknown reason clutched it tightly to her breast. A short but fervent prayer for the safety of her daughter was offered up as she felt the heat of her own tears begin to burn her cheeks.

A tap on the window startled her. She glanced in the rearview mirror and saw an old pickup truck parked directly behind the car, and as she rolled down the window an old man with weathered features and a kindly smile looked in on her. At his side was a woman about the same age and obviously his wife.

"You folks having some trouble?" the old man asked.

"Yes, oh, yes, thank you for stopping." A feeling of relief washed over her as she heard the man's voice and realized she was not alone. "My daughter is very ill and the car's broken down. Can you help me?"

It was a plea more than a question and the woman responded immediately.

"Here," she said, "you come out here and show Dad what's wrong with the car and I'll take care of your little one."

The arrival of the couple, startling though it was, had given Ruth a calm sense of assurance. Quickly she got out of the car and let the old woman slip in in her place. With a sense of complete assurance the woman took Becky into her arms and put her cool hand on the feverish brow.

"Ummm, that's a nasty fever," she said soothingly. "Is your tummy still hurting?"

Becky looked up at her, eyes wide with surprise. "Did my mommy tell you?" she asked.

"You're going to be all right for now," the woman continued, ignoring Becky's question. "Your mommy needs to get you to a doctor, but you'll be fine till then, okay?"

The woman's soft voice and gentle touch seemed to calm Becky down completely. She relaxed against the woman's breast as the pain in her stomach turned into a steady throb.

A moment later the hood on the car slammed shut.

"That should keep you going for a bit," the man said. "Just head straight on into town and don't stop till you come to the hospital. It's a big building, first right turn as you get into town. You can't miss it."

"Thank you very much," Ruth replied. "I'm lucky you came along."

The woman carefully laid Becky's head against the car seat and slipped out.

"Your little one's resting fine," she said. "She'll be all right till you get into town. But you have to take her right to the hospital, dear. Do you understand?"

"Yes, yes." She paused, tears in her eyes. "I don't know how to thank you," she said.

"Don't even try, miss," the woman said with a smile. "Just get the little one in to the doctor. Hurry, now."

Ruth climbed quickly under the wheel, turned the key, and felt the engine come to life. She turned to wave to her benefactors once more, but . . . they were gone. She glanced in the rearview mirror. The old truck was gone too. As suddenly as they had arrived they had disappeared. Ruth could see no side road they could have turned onto, no foliage or trees to obscure them in any direction. They seemed simply to have vanished.

The sudden appearance and just as sudden disappearance of the old couple nagged at her, but right now she had more important things to tend to. She dropped the transmission into drive and sped toward Cedarvale. She would say later that she didn't even think of touching the brake until she'd pulled up in front of the hospital.

Several hours later, with Becky resting comfortably in a hospital bed, sleeping off the effects of the anesthetic and her appendectomy, Ruth had a chance to relax and talk with the doctor who had performed the operation.

"Your daughter is going to be fine," he told her confidently.

"We were lucky, I guess," Ruth replied.

"You don't know how lucky," the doctor said. "With the condition her appendix was in, believe me, it's a miracle it didn't burst."

Two days and one phone call later Harry was standing in the hospital corridor waiting for Ruth and a nurse to bring his daughter to him. As soon as she was certain Becky would be all right, Ruth had called the camp and Harry was granted emergency leave. A military plane had flown him to Alamogordo and from there he caught a ride on a tanker truck going to Cedarvale. *Someday,* he thought, *I'll ask her how she got out here, but not today.*

A local mechanic had replaced the pulley on the car after assuring both Ruth and Harry that there was no way any car could run for more than thirty seconds without that particular device. He thought it was a miracle that the thing had held together until she stopped at the hospital. Ruth was beginning to understand just how miraculous the whole event had been. When she told the mechanic about the old man fixing it for her out on the road the mechanic just shook his head.

"Somebody might have fixed something for ya," he told her with an air of finality, "but it wasn't that pulley."

Ruth just paid the bill and let it drop. No point in trying to explain that she had examined the broken pulley herself.

Harry was having a hard time understanding why he couldn't just go to her room and get Becky, but the doctor assured him it would be better if he waited. Soon a nurse pushing a wheelchair came into his view. Ruth walked alongside as Becky rode comfortably, holding her favorite toy, a music box with a broken angel on top.

"Hey, there's my girl," Harry announced as he rushed up to her.

"Daddy!" Becky shouted, turning to the nurse. "That's my daddy."

"I'll take it from here," Ruth said.

The nurse smiled, patted Becky on the head, and walked away.

"See, I told you I had a surprise for you," Ruth said.

"Oh, Mommy, this is the best surprise ever."

Harry reached out with both arms and lifted Becky gently to his chest. "I'm so glad to see you, sweetheart," he whispered. "You gave me quite a scare."

"I'm sorry, Daddy, but . . ."

Harry was turning her slowly in the hallway and in the process had brought her around to where she could see a wallful of pictures that stretched out along the corridor. Becky's eyes fell on one of them and she pointed at it and began pulling at her father to turn around and see.

"What is it, sweetheart?" He turned slowly to follow where she was pointing.

"Look, Mommy," Becky cried, "it's them, it's the people that helped us."

Ruth walked over to the wall for a closer look. The man was wearing a suit and the woman was also in her Sunday best, quite a change from the overalls and cotton print they had been wearing out on the road, but it was the same couple, no doubt about it.

Ruth turned to the doctor. "This couple," she asked, "—do you know where we could find them? I'd really like to thank them properly."

The doctor just stared at the young family standing there in front of him. Ruth had told him about the old man and woman who had stopped on the road to help her, but this couldn't possibly be.

"Doctor?" Ruth asked again.

"Uh, I'm sorry Mrs. Linden, are you saying this is the couple who stopped to help you?" The doctor indicated the same photograph Becky was pointing at.

"Yes. They're dressed differently, but that's definitely the couple."

"Mrs. Linden," the doctor said, "read the inscription."

Ruth turned back to the photograph and read the small gold plate mounted on the bottom of the frame. *A donation has been made to this hospital in loving memory of my parents . . .*

Harry and Ruth looked at each other, then turned back to the doctor. "What does that mean?" Ruth wanted to know.

"Well, Mrs. Linden," the doctor replied, "all the pictures on this wall are of patrons of the hospital. Some are still living, but some, like this couple, have had donations made in their behalf after they died. Mr. and Mrs. Hollander here, they've been dead since 1949."

"Thank you, doctor," Ruth said softly as she gathered up Becky's things. "I guess we'd better be going now."

Outside, in the warm New Mexico sun, Ruth stopped and looked back up the road toward Highway 54. "It was them," she said to her husband. "I don't know how, but it was that old couple that stopped and helped us and saved Becky's life." She turned to look her husband right in the eye and repeated, "It was them."

For Ruth and Becky all their questions had been answered. The sudden appearance and disappearance of the old couple, Becky's fever and pain going away, the car working in spite of the broken pulley. Ruth's silent prayer had been answered.

There was a long pause as Harry looked into the faces of his wife and daughter. Both of them looked as if they had just seen an angel.

"C'mon," he said softly. "I found a beautiful little house that I can't wait for you to see."

Harry Linden quickly got used to seeing his daughter's little angel music box in a place of prominence on the mantelpiece of their new home. And over the next few years he became aware of a number of serious works written about guardian angels. People and cultures all over the world tell myriad stories about them.

Reports about guardian angels invariably say that when they appear to people in need, they do not wear white gowns or come fitted out with wings. To the contrary, they are said to take the most ordinary forms and wear things like cotton prints and bib overalls, just like folks in Cedarvale, New Mexico. That's certainly the way Harry and Ruth and Becky Linden describe them.

PART II

IN SEARCH OF
SELF AND
SELFLESSNESS

≈≈≈

Let's move on to our second category: miracles that bring about personal growth.

One of the more interesting things that I uncovered in the preparation of this book is that while many, perhaps even most, of the miracles and wonders that I encountered deal to some degree with matters of life and death, not all of them have that specific purpose. Sometimes, it seems, a life is saved, so that another life might be changed or enlarged upon.

Seen in another light, these lives are also saved; saved from the prison of selfishness and the destructiveness of pride. The events that produce such lifesaving consequences are frequently more subtle. There is hardly ever a sudden flash of insight or a blinding light that shows a new direction. No, in these instances the change takes place over some period of time. Quite often the person affected isn't even aware of what is taking place. Indeed, that seems to be part of the miracle.

Wonderful things happen to some people, I am convinced, for no other reason than to help them grow within themselves and become better people, better neighbors, better friends.

CHAPTER 6

ONE GOOD TURN

≈≈≈

Unlike old dogs, human beings can indeed be taught new tricks. Most of us do change and grow throughout our lives. The challenge, it seems, is to change and grow with purpose; to do it in such a way that we can help make the world or our town or just our neighborhood a little better place.

For most people that just sort of happens as they come in contact with new people, new situations, and new responsibilities. There are some, however, who seem to need a little push in the right direction.

Al and Jackie Miller loved living in the city. They were young, upwardly mobile, as that term is used these days, and black. He was in his early thirties, a successful writer for a small advertising agency and bent on enjoying the fruits of his labor. She was in her late twenties, held a supervisory position with the phone company, and believed that one of the reasons to work hard and get a bigger apartment was to make room for a growing family. In this latter regard Al and Jackie did not see eye to eye.

One warm Saturday afternoon Al and Jackie decided to go apartment hunting. Their discussions about increasing the size of their family always wound up floundering on the shoals of Al's sense of me, my, and mine, so Jackie decided to take another tack. She suggested they look for a bigger apartment in a more "upscale" neighborhood. Al jumped at the idea.

The fact was that Al Miller had made a Maypole out of the first-person personal pronoun, and he spent much of his time just looking for excuses to dance around it. Few of his sentences began with anything other than the letter *I*. To call Al ambitious, impatient, and frankly self-centered would not be far off the mark. Jackie loved him, but she realized, too, that he was becoming a boor.

The Millers had just come out of an apartment house in a neighborhood that wasn't quite up to what Al had decided was his standard, and he was anxious to move uptown. Jackie was scanning the listings in the real-estate section of the paper they had brought with them and wanted to look at a few more apartments in the immediate area. The discussion was still going on when Marsha Givens walked up to the crosswalk where Al and Jackie were standing waiting for the light to change and arguing about which direction to go next.

Marsha was a plain woman, probably in her early thirties, and just a little bit preoccupied. In fact Marsha Givens seemed a little bit preoccupied most of the time. A true earth-mother type, she had never married, but she loved children and spent much of her time working with gifted but disadvantaged youngsters from all over the city.

Al didn't know any of this, of course; he just looked up from the paper and saw her start to step into the street in front of a car that had no intention of stopping. In that instant Al Miller made the move that would change his life forever: he leapt forward, grabbed Marsha Givens around the waist, and pulled her back out of the path of the oncoming car.

The driver belatedly saw the woman and slammed on his brakes, screeching to a stop and barely missing the two bags of groceries that Marsha had been carrying when Al's sudden rescue sent them crashing to the ground.

Marsha looked at the car and swallowed hard. Then she turned to look at her benefactor.

"Thanks," she said, her voice quavering slightly, "that was close. I owe you."

"No, that's okay," Al replied. "Sorry about the bags."

The driver of the car glared at the trio standing on the curb, cursed, and drove away as Marsha bent down to try and salvage what she could from her shopping trip.

"Here, let me give you a hand," Jackie said, stooping to pick up a can of corn and what was left of a bag of potatoes.

"Oh, thanks," Marsha replied. "It's my own fault, really. I told them not to use double bags. Why kill another tree, right?"

Al looked on with growing frustration as the two women gathered up what they could in their arms. Jackie saw that there was no way they were going to be able to carry all of the items they could retrieve, so she just started handing things to Al. He glared at her as each new item dropped into his arms but he said nothing.

"Why don't we just help you carry these things?" Jackie volunteered. "You'll never make it by yourself."

"Thanks again," Marsha said. "My apartment's just across the street."

The two women started across the street as soon as the light changed. Al rolled his eyes toward the heavens, muttering something about not having time for this kind of Boy Scout crap, but he dutifully followed.

"You folks looking for an apartment?" Marsha asked.

"Yes, as a matter of fact we are." Jackie was obviously surprised. "How did you know?"

"Not too many people stand around on the street corner discussing real estate ads unless they're looking for an apartment."

Jackie laughed. "No sense in being subtle about it, is there?"

They turned down the walkway into Marsha's apartment building, Al reluctantly following with his armload of cans and fresh vegetables.

"This is a great neighborhood," Marsha said. "I hope you find a place. You'd really like it around here."

Just as they reached the main entrance of the building the door opened and the apartment manager came out. She recognized Marsha immediately and held the door open for them. As they made their way inside Marsha noticed that the manager was holding an APARTMENT FOR RENT sign in her hand.

"Oh, Joan," she said brightly, "if something's opened up in the building, these people are looking for an apartment."

Al grimaced, but Marsha quickly turned to Jackie and added, "If something has opened up in this building, you really should check it out."

It was quite a scene. Jackie was inside, the real-estate listings jammed into her pocket, her hands full of potatoes, a box of corn flakes under one arm and a roll of paper towels under the other. Joan, the apartment manager, was outside, holding the door open with one hand and clutching the brand-new FOR RENT sign with the other. Al was facing the apartment manager with his arms full of cans and boxes, wondering if maybe he wouldn't have been better off to just let Marsha step in front of that car. And Marsha? Marsha was standing half in, half out of the door, trying her best to match everyone up.

There was a long, awkward silence. Finally Joan spoke up. "My name is Joan," she said, "the apartment manager. We have a two-bedroom that just became vacant, if you'd like to take a look."

"Yes," Jackie said, just barely ahead of Al's "No, I don't think so."

Another awkward silence, during which Al had time to catch the withering look that Jackie fired in his direction.

"Well," he said, "as long as we have to go inside anyway, we might as well take a look." He paused, but nobody moved. "We are going inside, are we not?"

They all laughed—everyone but Al—and went on into the foyer. Up one flight was Marsha's apartment. Once the groceries were stacked on the table everyone felt a little more comfortable, especially the girls. By the time Al added his armload to the pile the three women were chatting away like long-lost friends.

Some might think it's only a slight coincidence that an apartment became available in this particular building the very moment Al and Jackie came along. Nothing could be farther from the truth. This pleasant Saturday would hereafter mark a special day in Al Miller's life. He was unaware of it at the time, but this was day one of the miracle that would change his life.

By the end of the month Jackie and Al Miller had not only moved into that building, they were on the same floor as their new "friend," Marsha.

After all was said and done, Al had to admit that it was a very nice apartment, the rent was reasonable, the commute downtown convenient, and the neighborhood as pleasant as Marsha had told them it would be. Jackie was thrilled, too, and even though they didn't often discuss it, Al knew that his wife was mentally redecorating that second bedroom as a nursery.

That, however, was not his biggest problem. His biggest problem was Marsha Givens, now friend, neighbor, and an ever-increasing responsibility. Somehow Marsha, single, a school librarian, and a little bit eccentric, always seemed to be getting herself into trouble. That might not have been so bad except that she always seemed to get in trouble at the very instant Al Miller walked by.

For example, there was the morning last week when Al came walking into the parking lot to find Marsha, a cardboard box full of canned food in her arms, standing there staring at a flat tire on her old Valiant.

Oh, no, not this time, he thought. He walked straight to his own car, opened the door, and tossed his briefcase inside, but it was too late. He had seen the pleading look in her eyes.

Muttering under his breath, Al tossed his jacket in on top of his briefcase and rolled up his sleeves as he walked over to where Marsha was standing.

"We're having a canned-goods drive at school for victims of the hurricane," she said apologetically. "This is the last day."

"Uh-huh," Al said. "You got a jack for this heap?"

"Yeah. It's in there somewhere."

Al took the box from her and set it on the ground while she fumbled in her purse for her keys. Twenty minutes later she was on her way and Al was heading back up to his apartment to wash up and change his shirt.

The part that irritated Al as much as anything was the fact that Marsha was such a do-gooder. She recycled everything, volunteered for community service, and even though her own life seemed to be on the very edge of coming unglued, she always had time to help others. This was not the sort of person Al Miller could understand.

"Thanks, that's another one I owe you." Al mimicked her gratitude as he stomped up the stairs. "I should be running a tab on this walking disaster," he muttered to himself. "I'd own this whole building by now."

He was still mumbling under his breath when he came back down and climbed in under the steering wheel of his own car. He looked at his watch, suppressed a swear word, and headed downtown a half hour late. *One of these days,* he vowed, *I'm just going to say no.* Funny part of it was that by the time he got to his office he was feeling pretty good. He couldn't quite put his finger on the reason why, but he felt good. Al was even kind of looking forward to explaining to his boss that he was late because he'd taken time to help a neighbor change a tire.

But that was just one example. At every turn with Marsha it was something new. Al could hardly get through a day, let alone a week, without there being some bit of help she appeared to need. And always it seemed as if Al were the only one there to help. Certainly Marsha didn't plan these things; still, Al had trouble believing it was all spontaneous. Even more confusing was the fact that Marsha never asked for his help. She was just there, in some kind of trouble, and always Al was presented with the same dilemma: ignore the situation, which he was inclined to do, or give her a hand, which is what he always did.

At first he was annoyed, even irritated, by what he felt was a forced generosity. Surely she must see that he didn't enjoy picking up her marbles every day. But as time passed, something changed, and although he would never admit it, that something was Al himself.

One Saturday morning, just as Al was tying the last knot on his jogging shoes, ready to head out the door, Jackie came rushing in.

"Oh, I'm glad I caught you," she said breathlessly. "Marcia's apart-

ment door won't open. She's with her group from the community center and one of them needs to . . . you know . . . make a pit stop."

"Why am I not surprised?" Al said, rolling his eyes toward the ceil-
ing. He shrugged his shoulders as if he were helpless against this continuing tide of good deeds and walked out the door.

Marsha, as I mentioned earlier, was not married. She regarded the
group of gifted children she worked with as "her kids," and spent as
much time with them as possible. She had "discovered" them, as she
liked to tell people, through a reading program she'd set up at the
inner-city community center. These kids were not merely bright, they
were gifted, and all of them came from broken or otherwise disadvantaged homes. Marsha took these special children under her wing. She
provided their curious and amazingly receptive minds with the stimula-
tion and inspiration of museums, concerts, and plays. In many ways she
was their best chance, perhaps their only chance, to reach their great
potential.

Al made his way through the small throng of eager youngsters and
tried the doorknob. It resisted as if it were locked, even though the key
was in the slot. Al tried to turn it with the key with the same result. Out
of the corner of his eye Al noticed one young girl all but in pain, trying
desperately to hold back one of nature's imperatives.

"This might take a minute," he whispered to her. "Why don't you go
over there to my apartment?"

The girl sighed audibly and turned around and dashed for his door.
Al smiled and went back to the task at hand.

It took a bit of doing. He had to move the key slowly in and out of
the lock, turning the knob back and forth as he did so, but finally there
was a click and the mechanism turned freely.

"I owe you one . . . again," Marsha said, as the kids pushed by him
into the apartment.

"Yeah, sure, I know." He turned and started down the stairs. As he
reached the bottom step he tossed back, "One of these days I'm gonna
collect." Al had no way of knowing how true that was.

Several days later the Millers were down in the laundry room. While
waiting for the machines to finish their work, they were revisiting the
same old argument they had had a hundred times before.

"Sometimes I don't think you want to have kids at all," Jackie complained.

"Hey," Al responded icily, "worse things could happen."

"Maybe," Jackie replied, obviously stung by his reply, "but I can't
think of a worse thing *not* to happen."

They were interrupted as Joan came down the stairs and headed for one of the dryers.

"Hi, there," she said pleasantly. "Everything working out okay in the apartment?"

"Yes," Jackie said, throwing Al an angry glance, "everything in the apartment is just fine."

Al started to say something but thought better of it. He picked up the laundry basket and placed it firmly next to one of the machines, but when he opened the lid he found it full of somebody else's clothes.

"Oh, I'm sorry," he said, turning to Joan, "are these yours?"

"No"—the apartment manager's shoulders drooped—"they've been there a couple of days. Probably belong to Marsha." She walked over and looked into the machine, adding, "She gets so busy sometimes, she just forgets the clothes are down here." Joan walked back to her own machine and started shoving coins into the slot as if she were angry. "Marsha's a real nice person," she said, on the verge of tears. "It's really too bad."

The tone of her voice and her strange attitude made Jackie suddenly apprehensive.

"Too bad?" she asked. "What do you mean?"

"Oh, it's just that she does so much for everybody else . . . it just makes me mad that she's the one that . . ." Her voice trailed off.

"That she's the one that what?" Jackie prompted.

Joan started the machine and picked up her empty basket. "I thought she might have told you, you seem like such good friends."

"Told us?" Al chimed in, suddenly interested. "Told us what?"

"Cancer! Marsha has pancreatic cancer. It's terminal. And it's a real shame."

Joan walked back up the stairs, leaving Al and Jackie staring at each other in numbed silence.

Later that night in the apartment their mood was still one of somber incredulity. They had gotten so used to seeing Marsha bustling in and out of the apartment carrying boxes and bags or herding some of "her kids," the thought that someday soon she might not be there just didn't want to take hold.

"That news about Marsha," Jackie said as she slipped under the covers, "—I just can't get it out of my mind."

"Yeah, me too." Al sat down on the edge of the bed.

"I keep thinking about how at first you didn't want to help her"— Jackie reached over and touched his arm—"but every time you turned around, there she was with another problem."

Al looked down at his hands and shook his head. "And every time I got sucked into fixing it."

"You know what?" Jackie continued. "For all your moaning and groaning and complaining, you like it."

Al flipped out the light and slipped under the covers beside his wife. "No way," he said firmly.

"It's true," Jackie insisted, "—just like the time you ended up driving all those kids from the community center to the zoo when her car broke down. You came home complaining, but you kept talking about the trip and the kids all through supper."

"C'mon. All I said was that the kids had a good time."

"Right. And it took you two hours to tell me that?"

Jackie turned on her side. She could just make out his face in the darkened room. "You know, every time you came back from doing something for her, you came back a little different, a little happier." She slipped an arm across his shoulders and waited for a response.

There was a long pause. Finally Al said, "you're dreaming. Get some sleep."

Jackie snuggled up closer to him. "I love you," she whispered, "I always have. But I want you to know that since we moved in here I'm finding more and more things to love about you."

Things continued on around the apartment house pretty much the same way they always had, over the next several months. Marsha didn't say anything to the Millers about her problem and they didn't think it appropriate to ask. Both Al and Jackie were aware, however, that they were seeing less and less of Marsha. In fact, when it came time for them to leave for a two-week trip to Chicago to visit Jackie's parents, they hadn't seen her for several days.

They were still unloading bags from the trunk of the car on their return from their trip when they noticed Joan standing in the entryway to the parking area with a couple they had never seen before. They were close enough to overhear her conversation.

"I can't get the painters in till next week," she told the man, "but it should be available by the first of the month."

The apartment manager turned and held the door open for the pair as they made their way back inside. Jackie hurried over in time to catch Joan before the door closed behind her.

"Joan?" she said, fearing the worst. "Has somebody moved out?"

The look on Joan's face told her her fears had been realized. "Marsha," she said, fighting back tears, "—Marsha died a few days after you left."

Al had come up to join the two women, but he quickly turned away when he felt the tears come to his eyes.

In the silence that followed, a hundred questions thundered through his mind. Why her? Why now? Why so suddenly? What about her kids? It was that last question that really tugged at him. In his most quiet moments Al realized the news of Marsha's death had affected him far more than he could ever have anticipated. And even though he had no way of knowing it at the time, Al Miller's business on this earth with Marsha Givens was far from over.

It was several nights later. The pillow talk in the Miller apartment turned once again to the subject of Marsha Givens.

"I really miss her," Jackie sighed.

Al turned on his side, his face away from her. "Believe it or not," he said, "so do I." There was a long silence and suddenly Al turned over on his back. "Those kids from the community center," he said, "—I wonder what's going to happen to them?"

"I don't know," Jackie replied sleepily. "Maybe somebody will come along."

She drifted off to sleep, but Al was having difficulty putting his thoughts about those kids to rest. At three A.M. he looked at the clock, moaned, and tried once again to get his mind and body to accept the idea of sleep.

Perhaps he had finally drifted off, or maybe he had just succumbed to fatigue and was stranded somewhere between sleep and waking. Wherever he was, he was abruptly aware of a shadow sweeping past the bedroom door into the hallway. Al sat up on the edge of the bed and rubbed his eyes. It was more something he felt than something he saw, and as he stood up to go investigate he realized that whatever was going on was not meant to frighten him.

At the bedroom door he stopped and looked down to the end of the hall. There was nothing there.

This is nuts, he thought to himself. *I've got to get some sleep.*

"There's no time to sleep."

Al spun around and looked at the bed. Jackie was still dead to the world. But he had heard a voice and that voice had said, "There's no time to sleep." He looked back into the hall and there, standing in the half-light afforded by the undraped kitchen window, he saw Marsha Givens. Instantly he recognized that it had been her voice he had heard.

"Marsha," he stammered. "How . . . ?"

"You've got to come, Al, right now."

Al didn't know what was happening, but he recognized the urgency in her voice and followed after her. When she reached the apartment door Marsha turned once more to make sure he was following, then opened the door and hurried out into the main hallway.

"I've got to be dreaming this," Al muttered to himself, but he followed her nevertheless.

As Al stepped into the hallway he caught one last glimpse of Marsha as she disappeared in a cloud of thick smoke. His eyes stung and he coughed convulsively. This was no dream. The building was on fire.

The image of Marsha faded from his mind as he rushed back into his own bedroom and shook Jackie awake.

"Wha . . ." she stammered, angry at first at his rough treatment.

"Jackie . . . get up! Now! We've got to get out of here."

The acrid smell of smoke hit her nostrils and she jumped up immediately. When they got back to the hallway Al pointed Jackie toward the stairs and gave her a gentle push.

"Hurry," he said.

Jackie realized Al was hanging back and stopped. "Come on!" she cried.

"No," Al said, "for some reason the alarm isn't working. You get down to the first floor and wake up Joan. Call the fire department. I've got to get everybody out of here."

Al turned and dashed down the hallway into the smoke. Jackie could hear him pounding on doors and shouting as she made her way down to Joan's apartment. A few months earlier she would have been stunned at the idea of Al Miller risking his life to save others, but on this night it seemed to her like precisely the thing her husband would do.

By the time the firemen arrived Al had been successful in waking all the other tenants and getting them out of the building. He was standing next to Jackie, watching the firemen wield their hoses and bring the fire under control, when Joan came up to him.

"I want to thank you," she said. "Helping everybody get out like that probably saved a lot of lives tonight."

Al continued to stare at the building. The experience that had woken him up was now coming back to his mind and the implications of it were staggering. He could almost hear Marsha's voice again. "That's another one I owe you," she would have said. Al smiled. He knew he had just collected the full debt.

"I still don't understand," Joan continued. "What made you get up and go out into the hall? How did you know there was a fire?"

"It's a little hard to explain," Al said quietly, bringing Jackie into a close embrace. "Right now I'd just like to make sure everybody from the building is all right."

Jackie put both arms around her husband and held him tightly. The tears that stained her face were not caused by the smoke from the fire.

Things got back to normal very quickly around the apartment building. In spite of all the smoke Al and Jackie's early warning had alerted the fire department in time to prevent the fire itself from doing a great deal of damage.

Getting back to normal also meant that the apartment manager began to see the kids from the community center going in and out on a regular basis once again. That hadn't happened since Marsha died. It didn't take her long to discover that it was Al Miller who was responsible. When she asked him about it one day he just shrugged and told her he was sure Marsha would have wanted someone to keep the lights turned on for these kids and he always had a little spare time.

Not many months after that Joan noticed something else about the Millers. Al had traded his car in on a minivan so he could get more kids to more places more often. One afternoon, as the van started to pull out of the driveway, the apartment manager saw Jackie rush out, waving and shouting. The group had started to leave without the lunches she had so carefully prepared for them. That, in and of itself, wasn't too surprising, but when she turned to walk back into the building Joan noticed that Mrs. Miller was decidedly pregnant.

Finally, some wondrous power had brought things full circle. One formerly selfish man had been literally forced by circumstance to reach out and help a woman in need, and he had discovered that deep down, it felt good.

Marsha Givens, who could no longer provide the love and attention her deserving special children needed, must have thought that Al Miller was a perfect candidate to take over the job, even if it took a miracle. We suspect she also knew that he sorely needed a lesson in giving and loving.

One final note. In less than a year little Marsha Miller was born.

CHAPTER 7

THE SILENT HITCHHIKER

≈≈≈

W<small>E OFTEN HEAR OF THE "MIRACLES OF MODERN MEDICINE." USUALLY</small> these "miracles" are splashed across the front page of the newspaper in bold headlines: S<small>URGEON</small> R<small>EPLACES</small> S<small>EVERED</small> H<small>AND</small>," or, the one I remember most vividly, POLIO ERADICATED. There is one family of doctors, however, who know that miracles in the medical profession often come in very different ways.

Dr. Benjamin Powell was a third-generation doctor. He had graduated, with honors, from the same medical school where his father and his grandfather had both excelled. But unlike his forebears, who were both general practitioners ("family practice," they preferred to call it), Benjamin had chosen to devote himself to medical research. His heroes were Pasteur, Koch, and Jonas Salk. Somewhere in the future were cures for cancer, heart disease, emphysema, and a hundred other debilitating diseases. Dr. Benjamin Powell wanted his name to be among those who would bring that future closer to the present.

Dr. Powell's dedication to this branch of medicine had created a few tense moments between himself and his father, but it was his grandfather who wouldn't let the argument rest. The doctors, nurses, and technicians at the lab where Benjamin Powell spent virtually all of his waking hours had grown used to seeing the sprightly seventy-five-year-old bustling down the corridor to his grandson's office. He never stayed very long, but hardly a week went by that the gleaming chrome-and-computer-infested laboratory wasn't graced by the slightly rumpled presence of the eldest Dr. Powell.

The young Dr. Powell was hardly surprised when his secretary, Rachel, buzzed to tell him his grandfather was in the building.

"Thank you, Rachel," he said without looking up from his computer.

A few minutes later the elder Dr. Powell poked his head in the door. "Not interrupting anything important, am I?" he asked rhetorically. "Don't see any patients waiting or anything."

Benjamin hit the "save" sequence on his computer and turned to the old man with a smile. "There are things besides patients that are important," he said, standing up to give his grandfather the obligatory hug.

"Humph!" was the only response.

"Well," Benjamin said, indicating the chair next to his desk, "what brings you by today, as if I didn't know?"

His grandfather sat down and began scanning the office as if he had never seen it before. It was sort of a ritual with the old man. His grandson had asked him about it once and his grandfather had told him he was just trying to find something that looked like a doctor's office. This time his eyes came to rest on the computer screen.

"I don't know how you can sit there and stare at that thing all day," he said impatiently. "What are you going to find in there, another miracle cure?"

"Who knows?" Ben replied good-naturedly. "We just work and hope."

Make no mistake about it, Benjamin Powell the Third had great respect for his grandfather and his father. He admired their dedication and tried very hard to emulate it. He kept abreast of all the latest techniques and could hold up his end in any discussion of basic medical practices. The only departure from family tradition came in the focus of the young doctor's dedication.

"Benjamin," his grandfather snapped, "you've been out of medical school for six years now. When are you going to practice real medicine?"

"Ah," the young doctor replied with a grin, "you have found a wonderful opportunity for me. Let me guess. It's a small clinic in Emmet, Idaho, and they desperately need a doctor willing to start at the bottom and work up."

His grandfather brushed aside the cynicism. "Actually, he said, "what I have in mind is much better than that." He paused just long enough to make sure his grandson was paying attention. "I'm talking about a volunteer mission."

"Whaaaat? I just—"

The old man had anticipated his reaction and brushed it aside. "Your father and I," he continued, "and several other *real* doctors, are going to set up a facility in Guatemala, and train some of the locals to work with the Indians in the remote villages. Could be a very rewarding way to spend the next six months of your life. We're holding a spot for you on the team. Who knows, you might get to do some meaningful research."

Benjamin leaned back in his comfortable chair and shook his head. "I know you don't believe it, Grandfather, but doing this kind of research *is* meaningful. And whether you ever admit it or not, it is also practicing medicine." He paused to let the weight of that sink in, then added, "besides, someone has to figure out what all that junk does you pill pushers give out."

Benjamin's grandfather recognized that the joke was meant to steer the conversation in another direction, but he had come there prepared to give his grandson a pep talk, and he was determined to give it.

"Heaven knows," he said, gesturing at all the machinery in the room, "I've got nothing against research. But working face to face with patients, with people who need your help—people who come to you believing in your knowledge and your skills—that's what medicine is all about. It's holding the hand of a frightened child and knowing there's a mother on the other side of the door praying for you. Something happens, something unexplainable, but more real than anything else you'll ever experience in your life."

The old man shifted in his chair and young Benjamin knew he wasn't quite through yet. "You can't find what I'm talking about in that computer, Benjamin"—he leaned forward for emphasis—"and I'm terribly afraid you're going to miss it."

Their eyes locked and Benjamin felt, once again, the depth of his grandfather's passion for medicine. "I know," he said quietly. "You never fail to remind me." Both men stood up. "What was it you said last time? 'Hands-on is medicine, everything else is just practice.'"

"Good, you remembered," his grandfather said, giving him a healthy pat on the back. "Now remember this: Saturday evening at the house . . . we'll be reviewing our plans with the other volunteers. We'd like to see you there."

Benjamin turned to walk out with him. "Oh, I'm sorry, Granddad. I'd like to come, really, but I'm committed to speak at a symposium in Lake Tahoe Saturday."

The older man sighed, obviously disappointed, but not discouraged. "What ever happened to that doctor's bag I gave you when you graduated from medical school?"

"It's in my car," Benjamin replied. "I always carry it with me."

They were at the door of the lab. The old doctor reached out and took his grandson's hand in a firm grip. "There are more miracles in that black bag," he said, emotion creeping into his voice, "than you'll ever find in that computer."

The two men parted, as they always did, with feelings of love and respect.

The following Saturday afternoon Dr. Benjamin Powell walked casually out of his fashionable home in Walnut Creek and climbed into his Mercedes and started up 680 to the I-80 junction. The system had been good to Dr. Powell. He enjoyed all the trappings of a successful career, the respect of his peers, money, even a certain degree of fame. He probably wasn't giving much thought to the black bag in the trunk of his car as he started the long climb up the mountain toward Lake Tahoe.

Before this day was over, however, the young doctor would have ample opportunity to remember his grandfather's words. Amazing events were about to occur in Dr. Powell's life, events neither he nor anyone else could ever have anticipated.

Winding up I-80 the doctor suddenly remembered some dictation he had left on the machine at the office. He had meant to tell Rachel to be sure and have it transcribed before he got in on Monday morning, but in the press of other business it had slipped his mind. He wasn't sure his cellular phone would work at this distance but he decided to give it a try anyway. He lifted the phone from its cradle between the two front seats, pushed the appropriate button, and in a moment he heard the familiar dial tone.

So far, so good, he thought as he punched in his office number. He was pretty sure no one would be there on a Saturday afternoon, but Rachel always checked the answering machine first thing every morning.

There was a click in the receiver and the recorded message came on: "This is Dr. Benjamin Powell's office. No one is here to take your call right now. Please leave a message and someone will return your call as soon as possible." *Beep!*

"Hi, Rachel, this is Ben. I left some dictation on the machine. I would really appreciate it if you could get on it as soon as you come in on Monday. Also, there's an important appointment change I need you to make—" A sudden burst of static made him pull the phone away from his ear. Gingerly he put it back, found the static to be gone, and continued. "Sounds like I'm getting out of range, the signal's breaking up. I'm going to dial again."

Dr. Powell hit disconnect and pushed the button marked redial. There was a pause and a recorded voice came into his ear: "I'm sorry, your call cannot be completed. You are out of the service area."

Benjamin put the phone back in its cradle. At least he'd gotten the most important part of the message delivered. He would call down and finish it when he got to Lake Tahoe.

The road to Lake Tahoe from the Sacramento side is about forty miles of six-percent grade. For trucks and most cars the climb is a bit of a struggle, but the big engine of the Mercedes handled it without even breathing heavily. The doctor was coming up rapidly on slower-moving traffic when he thought he saw a young boy standing by the side of the road.

At first it was just a glimpse between cars that had to slow down before going around a big eighteen-wheeler, and he wasn't sure it was really what he thought it was at all. Then, as he shifted over into the outside lane, he could see the boy quite clearly. He looked to be not more than eight or nine years of age. He was dressed in what looked like a school outfit of some kind and one of those baseball-type caps that all young boys seem to have. As near as the doctor could tell, he was just standing there watching the cars go by.

It was odd, he thought, for a boy that young to be way up here by himself, and he kept a close watch on the youngster as the gap between them steadily closed.

There were just a couple of cars between the Mercedes and where the boy was standing when suddenly the boy turned and looked Dr. Benjamin Powell squarely in the eye. Almost automatically the small hand came up, thumb extended in the time-honored gesture of the hitchhiker.

Dr. Powell didn't ordinarily pick up hitchhikers, but there was something about this youngster that was immediately compelling. He was so young and so far away from . . . anywhere . . . that the doctor decided to make an exception. He pulled to the side of the highway and brought the car to a stop. When he glanced in the sideview mirror he saw the boy racing toward him on a dead run. Dr. Powell decided he must have been standing there a long time to be in such a hurry and reached across the seat to make sure the door would be open for him.

The boy climbed up into the seat, pulled the door closed with a jerk, and began to peer straight ahead through the windshield as if impatient to be going. Dr. Powell's earlier impression was now confirmed. The boy was neatly dressed in some kind of school colors. The cap on his head, however, was the familiar black and orange of the San Francisco Giants.

Dr. Powell released his foot from the brake, looked over his left shoulder, and moved back out into the traffic lane.

"Well," he said to the boy, "you're a bit young to be out hitching rides, wouldn't you say?"

The youngster looked at him intently without saying a word, then returned his attention to the road ahead, rocking forward and back as if impatient with their rate of speed.

"Okay, okay," the doctor said, "I'll pick it up."

They traveled a few minutes in silence and Dr. Powell decided to try again. "So," he asked, "do you have very far to go?"

The boy's attention was riveted on the highway. He didn't acknowledge the doctor's question with even so much as a look in his direction.

Great, Benjamin thought, *twelve years of medical school and I can't communicate with an eight-year-old.*

Dr. Powell was about to pull out into the left lane of traffic to go around another car when the boy reached over and grabbed his sleeve and began pulling on it while pointing to an off ramp a few hundred yards ahead.

"Is that where you're going?" he asked, hoping at last to get some response. The boy said nothing, but his level of agitation increased the closer they came to the turnoff.

"Okay," he said, "we'll go this way." Dr. Powell slowed down and made the turn. The boy was now on the edge of the seat, gripping the dashboard as if he thought he would fall out of the car if he let go, but his eyes never left the road. The turnoff led to one of those "ranch" exits that are rarely traveled.

Dr. Powell was not a man given to sudden impulses, yet here he was, impulsively following the silent directions of a young hitchhiker he had impulsively picked up. Not only that, he was beginning to feel very protective of the boy. Someone, he thought, is going to have some explaining to do for leaving him out here alone.

Suddenly the youngster all but stood up, pointing eagerly at the road immediately ahead. "Yeah, I see it too," the doctor said. Two heavy black skid marks had left a nasty scar on the road leading directly to a shattered guardrail at the beginning of a slow curve.

The Mercedes came to an abrupt halt in front of the guardrail and Dr. Powell jumped out to get a better look. What he saw made the breath catch in his throat. There, a hundred yards down the embankment, a small yellow-and-black school bus was lying on its side. The top of the bus was jammed up against a large tree trunk, which was probably the only reason it hadn't tumbled all the way down to the bottom of the canyon. The door of the bus was jammed against the ground, and through the window of the rear emergency exit Dr. Powell could see several children pounding against the glass and shouting at him.

From that point on everything became instinct, training, and skill. In what seemed like a single motion the doctor pushed the button that popped open the trunk lid, tossed his jacket into the backseat, and jerked the cellular phone from its cradle.

"One time," he whispered, "let this thing work."

To his amazement the dial tone exploded in his ear the instant he punched it on. Almost automatically he pushed his access number, followed by 911. He held his breath as he listened to the familiar ringing sound.

"This is nine one one. Your name, please."

The voice was clear as a bell. "Yes," he shouted into the phone, "my name is Dr. Benjamin Powell. I'm at the site of an accident on a side road south of I-80 about twenty miles west of Lake Tahoe. A small school bus has gone off the road and rolled over. Can you find us? We need an ambulance."

"I know where you are, Dr. Powell. We can—"

Benjamin didn't wait to hear the rest of the message. He raced around to the trunk of his car, grabbed the black bag and a couple of wool blankets he kept there just in case he ever got to go to a football game, and raced down the incline to the bus.

The emergency exit of the bus had been jammed shut in the crash. Finding strength he didn't know he had, the doctor braced his foot against the rear of the bus and jerked the door open. A small girl, probably not more than seven years old, tumbled into his arms crying. There was a thin trickle of dried blood running down one cheek, but the small cut had clotted over. Quickly he checked her over but couldn't detect any broken bones.

Several other children crowded past him, bruised, a bit dazed, all of them with cuts and scrapes but otherwise ambulatory. Except for signs of shock and a lingering fear, they seemed to be all right. Dr. Powell spread the blankets on the ground and told them to lie down. As he listened to himself talk to the children he was surprised at how calm he sounded. Inside all of his senses were accelerated as he touched a bruise, looked at a cut, or listened intently through the unfamiliar stethoscope. At least he knew for sure that these children could move. He would have to get back to them shortly and check more carefully.

"Don't worry," he said to one of the older children as he laid her head gently on the blanket, "I'm going to help you. I'm going to help all of you."

Dr. Powell turned his attention back to the interior of the bus. It looked like a house of horrors. Some of the seats had come loose and were lying crazily against what had been the roof of the bus. Backpacks were scattered everywhere. But worst of all, he could see four sets of arms and legs that weren't moving.

One by one he attended each child in the wreckage, determined they were alive, and carried them out to one of the blankets. He counted one broken arm, one fractured collarbone, a mild concussion, at least one broken leg, and lots of cuts and bruises, but they were all alive.

Dr. Powell was just bringing the last of the children from the bus when an ambulance and highway patrol car pulled up. One of the paramedics rushed up to take the child from his arms.

"Dispatch said you're a doctor, is that right?"

"Yes, yes, I am."

"Anybody else in there?"

"Just the driver. I didn't get to him yet."

The other paramedic had already started to escort the children who were able to move back up the hill toward the ambulance. When the two men came back down they were packing stretchers.

Dr. Powell explained the condition of each child to the paramedics as they were carefully lifted onto the carriers and taken to the top of the hill. As the last one was lifted up the doctor slipped the stethoscope from his neck, gathered everything back into his black bag, and followed along behind. He was suddenly very tired.

Back up on the road he had a chance to survey his work. The four children who had been injured the worst were all loaded aboard the ambulance and seemed to be resting comfortably. Other children were sitting in the patrol car and in the front seat of the ambulance. A few moments later a second patrol car arrived.

Dr. Powell walked over to his car and tossed the black bag into the trunk. As he did so he realized he had used just about everything in it. *Got to remember to resupply,* he thought. As he closed the trunk he caught a glimpse of himself in a reflection in the rear window. He was a mess. His silk shirt and tie were covered with blood and dirt and now that he had time to check, he discovered a large tear in one leg of his pants.

I won't be delivering any paper tonight, he thought, finally remembering Lake Tahoe and the symposium.

"Hey, Doc!"

Wearily, Dr. Powell turned to the sound of the voice. "Yes?" he said.

"I've got a young lady here wants to talk to you."

Benjamin walked over to where the paramedic was standing, holding the first little girl who had tumbled out of the bus into his arms. She had a bandage on the side of her head and on one knee, but she was smiling.

Dr. Powell reached out to touch her cheek, but the little girl caught his hand in hers and brought it to her lips. "Thank you for helping us," she said. "I'll remember you always."

There was an unexpected lump in his throat and he had trouble forming a reply. Finally he said, "And I'll remember you too. Every one of you."

The little girl surrendered his hand and he was turning to go back to his car when he saw another stretcher being brought to the top of the hill. The body on it was covered over. The medics, he noticed, had used one of his blankets.

"Is that the driver?" he asked, turning back to the paramedic who was holding the little girl.

"No, we brought him up a few minutes ago."

Dr. Powell looked back at the stretcher and realized his blanket was covering a much smaller form.

"But I thought"—the words stuck in his throat—"I thought I got all the children."

One of the highway patrolmen had been standing nearby and heard the conversation. "We thought you had, too, Dr. Powell, but when we removed the driver we found this one." He nodded toward the stretcher.

"But, how . . . I mean, what . . . ?"

"As near as we can figure out," the patrolman continued, "the driver had a heart attack. One of the children told us that this young boy grabbed the steering wheel and probably kept the bus from going all the way to the bottom of the ravine. But when the bus went over he was apparently crushed between the ground and the weight of the driver. Too bad. He was a real hero."

The stretcher came abreast of them and Dr. Powell reached out and stopped the men. "I'd like to take a look, if you don't mind," he said softly.

Slowly he lifted the corner of the blanket, revealing the face of a handsome young boy. He reached down and gently turned the face toward him. Dr. Benjamin Powell stared in disbelief. He turned and looked at the police officer his eyes wide with amazement.

"I know this boy," he said. "I picked him up on the highway. He's the one who brought me here, showed me the accident."

The highway patrolman and the medics exchanged glances but said nothing. Dr. Powell turned back to the stretcher to look more closely. There were smudges of dirt on the pale cheeks and the hair was mussed, but there was no doubt about it. This was the boy he had picked up hitchhiking. In all the frenzy of helping the other children he had completely forgotten about his silent passenger, but here he was.

Carefully, the doctor replaced the cover over the small face and watched as the two men carried him off. He wished the boy had spoken to him. He would like to have heard the sound of a hero's voice.

Puzzled and completely drained of energy he walked back over to his car. Remembering how well the phone had worked when he called for the ambulance he decided he would just call the lodge at Tahoe and let somebody there make his apologies. He slipped into the front seat and lifted the phone from its hook, pushed the talk button, and waited. There was nothing. No dial tone, no static, nothing. He sat there staring at the phone.

"Don't think you'll be able to use that up here." It was the highway patrolman.

"What?"

"Too mountainous and too far away from a transmitter," the patrolman said. "I'll be happy to relay a message for you on my radio if you'd like."

"But I used this to call you guys," Dr. Powell protested. "Why would it work then and not now?"

"Beats me." The highway patrolman shrugged and walked away.

Fatigue and confusion were beginning to take their toll. *Maybe I just imagined the whole thing,* he thought, and slipped the telephone into its cradle. But as he looked down to make sure the phone was seated properly his eye caught something protruding between the passenger seat and the center console. He reached down and gave it a tug. Slowly a small baseball cap emerged, black and orange, with the insignia of the San Francisco Giants on the front. It was just the right size for an eight-year-old boy.

Dr. Benjamin Powell looked at the cap and thought, how very appropriate. This had been a day of giant improbabilities. His uncharacteristic stop to pick up a hitchhiker, a 911 call that should not have connected, and now this irrefutable reminder that somehow, some way, the boy who died in that accident had, in fact, been a passenger in his car.

A few weeks later Dr. Powell's grandfather came to the lab to see him again. This time he was on a different mission.

Dr. Powell's office was neat and tidy. There were no papers on the desk or on the floor. Everything was placed in boxes or on shelves.

"It won't be the same here without you," Rachel said sadly.

"Thanks, Rachel, but things wouldn't be the same even if I stayed." Dr. Powell reached over and flipped the computer switch to off. "All of my notes and the computer disks are in the top file drawer," he said. "You know where everything else is located. If there's an emergency you can reach me here."

Dr. Powell handed her a small card. Printed in his own neat hand was the address and phone number of a health clinic in Guatemala.

"Should be nice there this time of year," Rachel said, trying to put the best face on things. "Be sure and write."

The scene was interrupted by the appearance of Benjamin's grandfather. "Ready, Doctor?" he asked with considerable pride.

"Yes, yes, I'm ready." Dr. Powell shook Rachel's hand, picked up a suitcase that was waiting by the door, and walked out into the corridor. Rachel watched until they had disappeared around the corner and started to close the door. Suddenly Dr. Powell reappeared.

"Sorry," he said, "I forgot something important."

He ducked inside the office and returned a moment later. In his hand was a boy's baseball cap. He folded it carefully and slipped it into his pocket.

Dr. Powell caught up to his grandfather once again and they continued down the corridor to the main entrance of the laboratory.

"Forget something important?" he asked.

Dr. Powell thought about it for a moment then said, "Do you remember what you told me . . . about special things happening when you—"

Dr. Benjamin Powell I held up his hand. "You don't have to tell me," he said. "I knew the minute you called and said you were coming with us." He paused to look in the face of his grandson. "Something happened when you found that school-bus wreck on the way up to Lake Tahoe, didn't it? Something very special, I mean."

"Yes. Something very special."

Grandfather Powell put his arms around the young doctor's shoulders and gave him a tight squeeze. "That's just the beginning, son, just the beginning. You'll see."

Dr. Benjamin Powell never tried to explain what had happened that afternoon on an isolated mountain road. When he told them about it both his father and his grandfather seemed to understand perfectly without any explanation at all. In the final analysis the most important thing about it to young Dr. Powell was simply the fact that it had happened . . . to him.

Dr. Benjamin Powell III just accepted the miracle for what it was, for how it changed him and for the understanding of his profession that it opened up, and for the kind of doctor it helped him to become.

PART III

THE MIRACLE OF FAMILY

≈≈≈

THIS NEXT CATEGORY IS ONE THAT HOLDS SPECIAL FASCINATION FOR ME and for most of the people I've talked to over the years about their miracles and other wondrous events. Interestingly enough, the older a family member is the less likely he is to describe the marvelous things that happen as miracles. Children have no problem with that definition at all. Perhaps there's more than we realize in the biblical admonition to become as little children.

One thing is certain: Of all society's institutions none is more durable or more important than the family. Families are the best hope of any community, state, or nation that is truly seeking to lift itself up to higher levels of peace and understanding. Without the family all other institutions of society fail.

It is perhaps not too surprising, then, that a watchful Providence would save some of the most fascinating miracles for families. Indeed, when you stop to think about it, the family itself is a miracle.

God, in his infinite wisdom, has provided a system whereby all of the energy that can be generated through the power of love and devotion is channeled into the hearts of young and old alike to keep the family strong and working together.

If, occasionally, families run into problems they can't handle by themselves, is it too farfetched to believe He might take a personal hand in helping things run a little more smoothly?

The families you are about to meet in these next chapters will all tell you they don't think it's very farfetched at all. In at least one instance, if he could talk, even the family dog would tell you that. But more about that in a moment.

Just about every man has dreams for his family. Some dream of happiness, some dream of success, and some even make the mistake of thinking happiness and success are the same thing.

Not all of our dreams come true, of course, but when one does come true, I mean literally come true, it is always a bit of a surprise. But maybe it shouldn't be.

CHAPTER 8

A FATHER'S DREAM

≈≈≈

Arnold Spencer sat at the kitchen table, newspaper in hand, a cup of coffee slowly cooling as he ignored it. Arnold usually read the morning paper with his coffee, but had found during the last few mornings nothing of sufficient importance there to keep his mind from drifting back to the dream he'd been having nearly every night.

It wasn't a particularly scary dream, it was just, well, perplexing.

"Are you off in dreamland again?"

"Hmmmm? Oh . . . yeah."

His wife, Grace, had disturbed his preoccupation and brought him back to the business at hand. He shook the paper a couple of times and started thumbing through it, looking for the sports section.

"That same dream again?" she asked.

"Uh-huh," he answered absentmindedly, "same one."

"Tell me again." Grace brought a cup of coffee to the table and sat down. "Maybe we can figure it out together."

Arnold folded the paper and set it aside. He tested the coffee for temperature with a careful sip, found it just about right, and took a full drink.

"Well," he said, leaning back in his chair, "it's like I told you before. I'm out in this no-man's-land, someplace I've never been before, or at least if I have, I don't recognize it."

"How about the fog?" Grace interrupted.

"Yes, the fog is there, thick and rolling up everywhere. Then maybe twenty or thirty feet away I see Louise. She's waving to me. Actually

≈ 91

it's more like she's motioning me to come to her. I start in her direction and she turns around and disappears into the fog. That's it."

"She isn't shouting or complaining or anything?"

"Nope." Arnold took another drink from his cup.

"That doesn't sound like our darling daughter," Grace said with a smile. "Are you sure it wasn't somebody else?"

As if on cue Louise Spencer, Grace and Arnold's sixteen-year-old daughter, came bouncing into the room.

"Hi, Mom. Hi, Dad. Gotta get some new shoes." She threw it at them as if it were all one sentence, and to add the exclamation point Louise dropped her not-quite-two-month-old sneakers into the wastebasket.

"Hey, hold it," Arnold cried. "I paid forty bucks for those just last month. They can't be shot already."

"Daddy"—her tone was patronizing and she looked at him as if she was certain he needed a brain transplant—"they're Ni-keeeees. Nobody wears Ni-keees anymore."

Arnold looked at Grace as if to say, *Are you gonna help me here?* but she just stood up and walked over to the sink.

"I thought we were talking about shoes?"

"Muh-thur!" There was that condescending tone once again, and now she was trying to bring Grace into the discussion on her side. "Will you please explain to Father the difference between Ni-kees and Ree-boks?"

Grace turned to face her daughter. The Spencer family lived well on what Arnold made as the sales manager of a fairly substantial manufacturing company. There were just the three of them; consequently Louise had always been given everything she wanted. Both parents were beginning to regret that generosity.

"I'm afraid you'll have to explain that one yourself," Grace told her. "The difference entirely escapes me."

"I don't believe this." Louise threw up her hands in exasperation. "You both must have grown up in the Dark Ages."

"Yes, well, let me throw a little light on this subject," Arnold said, retrieving the exiled sneakers from the wastebasket. "You can wear these until they wear out or I get my forty bucks' worth, whichever comes first."

Louise put her hands on her hips and glared at him. "Oh, sure," she said defiantly, "like I'm gonna wear shoes that have been in the trash." She turned and stomped out of the house.

Grace turned quickly back to the sink and tried to hide a smile. She didn't think Arnold would appreciate the humor she found in seeing him standing, openmouthed, in the middle of the kitchen, holding a pair of girl's sneakers. She was right.

"I don't see anything funny in this," he said, dropping the shoes on a chair. "She'll wear these or she can go barefoot."

"She will, you know," Grace replied.

"Will what?"

"Go barefoot." Grace walked up and straightened his tie before looking him in the eye. "I hate to admit it," she said, "but we are raising a little snob."

"No," Arnold snapped back, "we are raising a *big* snob."

Arnold Spencer, husband and father, was experiencing a parent's common dilemma. There are only so many years to raise and guide and influence one's children. Finding the perfect balance between giving them the things that will help them grow and become healthy, happy, adult human beings, and the things you want to give them just because you can, is the universal predicament of parenthood. There is always the fear that one day soon the children will be gone and you will have given them too much of one and not enough of the other.

Arnold didn't know it yet, but his strange recurring dream was trying to tell him he would have an opportunity to balance the scales.

One Saturday morning a few weeks later the second ingredient of the Spencer family miracle fell into place.

At twelve-fifteen Arnold picked up Louise at the mall, where she had been shopping with friends. Arnold watched the group as they came bustling out the main entrance, laughing and shoving one another. Louise seemed to be one of the leaders of the group, and for a moment his chest swelled with pride.

Louise quickly spotted the family station wagon, waved to her friends, and rushed over and jumped in. Arnold was about to pull away when he spotted Ruthie Caswell coming out the door. She was by herself, and when the other girls saw her they quickly turned away.

"Hey, there's Ruthie," Arnold said. "Should we give her a ride?"

"Naah, her mom's coming. Let's go."

Arnold was puzzled. "Louise," he said, "if Ruthie was here, why didn't you tell me and I'd have told her mother I'd pick you both up. I thought Ruthie was your best friend."

"Just because you live next door to someone doesn't mean you have to be friends," Louise snapped. "Besides, none of the other girls like her." She slumped back against the seat and refused to look in Ruthie's direction.

No question about it, Arnold's little girl had an attitude and Arnold didn't know what to do about it. His wife kept reminding him it was all in growing up, but Arnold was beginning to think it would take a miracle to get through to her.

On the way home Arnold decided to take a shortcut through a new housing development that was just getting under way. No one would be working, he was sure, and cutting through would save him a mile or so. Besides it gave him a chance to see if any new construction techniques were being used that he didn't know about.

They had just rounded a corner in the newest part of the development when Arnold spotted a pickup truck. That in and of itself wasn't too surprising, but the two men standing in back of the truck were obviously throwing something into the high grass and weeds next to the road. When they saw the station wagon they jumped back into the truck and drove hurriedly away. That pushed things way past Arnold's curiosity threshold and in spite of Louise's complaints he turned the station wagon to the right and drove over to the spot where the truck had been.

Arnold brought the vehicle to a stop, climbed out, walked around, and looked down into the grass and debris by the side of the road. There, lying among the splintered boards and waste of the construction site, was a small dog, its sides pumping painfully with every breath. He walked over and knelt beside the animal to get a better look. Arnold couldn't tell how old it was, but it was certainly no puppy. And he couldn't identify the breed. What he could see of the multicolored coat, underneath all the dirt and molt, gave him the impression that this little fella probably didn't have what you could call a "bloodline."

"Oooooh, yuk!" Louise had gotten out of the car and come over to see what her father found so fascinating.

Arnold just looked up at her and shook his head. If his mind hadn't been made up before, it certainly was now.

"Open up the back of the wagon," he said, reaching down and gently lifting the small dog from the ground.

"Daddy!" Louise fairly shrieked. "You're not going to put that awful-looking thing in the car?"

"Just get the door open," he said impatiently. "We've got to get this little guy to the vet."

Louise looked around as if maybe she'd rather walk home than ride in the same car with a dirty little dog, but at last she dropped the tailgate door of the station wagon, then hurried around to climb in the front seat before her father could ask her to actually touch the thing.

Arnold laid the dog down gently and made sure there was plenty of clearance before closing the door. It wasn't that he was such a dog lover; it was just that he hated to see anything suffer. There was no way he could leave the dog there to die.

A short time later at the veterinary hospital Arnold was having a hard time dealing with his daughter's impatience. He had been listening to a steady stream of complaints ever since picking up the dog, and his own patience was wearing thin.

"Louise," he said firmly, "we're going to wait until the doctor tells us what's wrong with that little dog, if it takes all afternoon. So just knock it off."

"But the game starts at two-thirty . . . and that dumb thing isn't even ours . . . it's just a—a—"

"Louise," he said in as stern a voice as he could muster with his daughter, "one more word and I'll leave you here and take the dog home."

A few minutes later the veterinarian, a tall young woman with her hair tied back in a neat bun, came into the waiting room.

"Well, Mr. Spencer," she said, "that little guy is in pretty bad shape. He's not a pup and he's been sick for a while. Looks to me like he's probably been starved and abused as well. If we can save him, and it's a big if, it could be expensive."

"What's the alternative?"

"Well, he's apparently been abandoned," she said sadly. "We'd have to put him to sleep."

"Can we go now?" Louise moaned.

Arnold was finding that his daughter's attitude was making it very easy for him to make up his mind.

"Tell you what," he said to the vet. "You fix him up, whatever it costs, and call me. He's got an owner now."

The veterinarian smiled and extended her hand. "Thank you, Mr. Spencer," she said. "We'll do everything we can for him."

"Good. Oh, by the way, Doc, can you tell what kind of a dog he is, or how old?"

"Well, he looks to be about seven or eight years old, but I'm afraid he's a variety all his own. Mostly terrier of some kind, but the ears look almost like a shelty." She paused for a moment then asked, "Why, does it make difference?"

"No, not at all," he said. "I was just curious."

"How old are you, Mr. Spencer?" the veterinarian asked.

"I'm forty-seven. Why?"

"In dog years," she said with a smile, "the two of you are just about the same age."

Five days and $140 later, the little stray dog was in his new home. A couple of shots, some tender, loving care, and the right amount of good food had quickly put him on the road to recovery.

Grace found herself quite excited about the idea of having a pet in the house. As a young girl growing up with three brothers she had gotten used to always having a dog around, but after she and Arnold got married the subject of pets just never came up.

When Arnold opened the kitchen door and let him in the house, the dog headed straight for Louise. She tried desperately to get out of the way but the animal was standing on his hind legs, pawing at her jeans and coaxing, as only a dog can coax, to be petted.

Grace smiled at her daughter's discomfort and immediately dropped to one knee and stretched out her hand. "Come here, fella," she pleaded. "Come on, let's get acquainted."

Immediately the animal dropped to all fours and raced over to sniff and lick the outstretched hand. "I think he likes me," Grace said, gathering the dog into her arms. "I think we'll be great friends."

"Yeah, well, *I've* got enough friends"—Louise sniffed—"and besides, he doesn't even have a name."

"Oh, yes," Grace said, releasing him to scamper about the room and check everything with his nose, "he must have a name."

Arnold watched as the dog jumped up into a small box bed he had fashioned earlier in the day. Grace had found an old pillow and covered it with terry cloth to put inside the box, and the dog took possession of it immediately.

"I'm open to suggestions," Arnold announced. "Anybody got any ideas for a name?"

"Considering the fact he'd be dead now if you hadn't coughed up a hundred and forty dollars for the vet," Louise said, "I think he ought to be called Lucky."

Arnold laughed. "Okay," he said, "that works for me. How about you, Grace?"

"I like it," she replied, "but let's ask him." She turned to look at the dog. "How about it, are you Lucky?"

The dog barked once and the name was sealed forever.

As the days passed, Lucky became part of the household, at least most of the household. Louise still threw a fit every time she came home and found him curled up with one of her stuffed toys. Once, when she walked in her room and found him smack dab in the middle of her bed, she let out such a shriek, even the stuffed giraffe jumped.

Over the next few weeks Lucky grew healthier and stronger. His fast recovery was most unusual for a dog his age. The vet even commented once that she thought it nothing short of a miracle.

Lucky quickly became part of the family and even though Louise tried hard not to show it, even she was developing an attachment for their new family member.

It was in this frame of mind that the family began preparing for their annual trip to visit Grace's sister in southern California. There had been considerable discussion as to whether or not they should take Lucky with them. Grace wasn't sure how her sister would take to having a dog around the house and Louise was positively apoplectic at the idea of having to drive five hundred miles sitting next to a dog. Arnold called the vet and made arrangements to board Lucky until their return.

The evening before their departure Louise was still finding things to gripe about. When her mother told her to set her alarm for six A.M. it was just too much.

"Don't growl at me," her mother told her. "Your father makes the travel plans."

Louise stomped out of the kitchen looking for her father and finally found him in the backyard tossing a stick for Lucky to fetch. It was a game the dog never tired of playing and one that Louise thought was perfectly inane.

Louise burst through the back door in full whine. "Why do we have to leave so early?" She groaned.

"Because we have to get Lucky over to the vet," Arnold explained, "and I want to get that out of the way early."

"You mean we have to get up in the middle of the night because of the *dog*?"

"Well," Arnold reminded her, "you didn't want him to come with us." He tossed the stick into a corner of the yard and Lucky raced over to get it. This time he brought it back and dropped it in front of Louise. She looked down into Lucky's pleading eyes, turned around, and stomped back into the house.

The next morning found them at the veterinary clinic bright and early. The vet was there to greet them and, as always, lavished most of her attention on the dog.

"We should be back late Wednesday afternoon," Arnold said, as he handed Lucky over.

Sensing something was different from their other visits, the dog started to whimper.

"Hey, it's okay, Lucky." Arnold reached over and began to scratch his ears. "We're only going to be gone a few days."

"It's all right, Lucky," the vet said adding her assurances as well, "—no shots or stitches this time, just a little stay in our hotel."

Somehow Lucky didn't seem reassured. He continued to whimper, but this time all it got him was a pat on the head and wave good-bye.

The Spencers made good time on the road and by ten-forty that morning they were a hundred fifty miles south of their home in Sacramento. Then just north of Fresno the southbound traffic began to get heavier.

Louise had tucked herself away in the backseat with a book and her Walkman stereo. Normally under those circumstances she wouldn't have noticed if a bomb went off. It may have been the sudden deceleration that got her attention but whatever it was, it was enough to make her sit up and look around a bit.

"What's goin' on?" she asked.

"Looks like we're getting into some fog," her mother replied.

"Just one of the rules of the road around here," her father added. "We almost always get fog around Fresno. Fifty, sixty miles south it'll be clear as glass."

The Central Valley of California is notorious for these seasonal fogs. Some of them shut down the interstate for hours. Driving in this area you can quite suddenly find yourself in an eerie gray world that closes in around you, reducing the entire universe to a circle of not more than twenty or thirty yards.

"I hate driving in this stuff," Grace said, peering anxiously into the gray soup on every side.

"Me too," Arnold replied, "but we're not far from the junction now. We'll have the worst of it behind us before long."

Louise sat back in the seat and took the earphones from her ears. It was something that had to be done every few hours if only to keep the circulation going to her head. But this time, as she dropped the headset into her lap, a familiar sound came to her ears. It was the sound of a dog barking, and not just any dog—it sounded like Lucky.

They were moving at a snail's pace one moment and then suddenly there would be a break in the fog and the traffic would immediately speed up. It was these sudden bursts of speed that created the greatest danger, but people somehow never seem to get the picture. At this precise moment they were traveling very slowly and Louise rolled her window down to see if she could hear more clearly. Suddenly she blinked, rubbed her eyes, and looked again.

"Mom," she shouted, "check this out."

Grace looked back over her shoulder to see what Louise was talking about. Then she, too, rolled down her window and stared out into the fog.

"Who does that look like to you?" Louise asked eagerly.

There, running alongside the station wagon and barking loudly, was a small dog that looked exactly like Lucky.

"Isn't that the strangest thing. . . ." Grace turned to her husband. "Arnold, you've got to see this."

"See what?" Given the circumstances Arnold was not about to take his eyes off of what little bit of the road he could see.

"It's a dog," Grace said. "It looks just like Lucky."

"That's nonsense."

"Daddy, it is Lucky, I know it is."

"It does look like him," Grace added, with some certainty.

Arnold started to protest but just then an off-ramp sign came into view and he decided to pull off the freeway. He needed a break anyway and he could let Louise satisfy herself that it was some dog other than Lucky. Besides, he knew if he didn't stop and check it out he'd hear about it all the way to Los Angeles and back.

A moment later the station wagon pulled to a stop at the side of the off ramp. Arnold turned on the emergency blinkers and got out and walked around the car. The fog limited his field of vision to not more than twenty feet as he tried to pick out the dog his wife and daughter assured him was there. Actually, he heard it before he saw it.

"I can't believe I'm doing this," he said, straining even harder to put an animal with the bark, but somewhere inside he had to admit the bark did sound familiar.

"Well, I saw it, and this dog looks just like Lucky," Louise insisted.

"Lucky," Arnold reminded them, "is locked in a kennel back at the vet's."

"I know," Louise said, "but maybe he got out somehow."

"Even if he did, we're two hundred miles from home."

Arnold was about to get back in the station wagon when he heard the bark again from somewhere in the fog.

"Lucky?" Louise looked down the embankment and saw the dog emerge from the gloom, walk straight toward her, and drop a small stick on the ground. "Dad, it's him, it's Lucky."

Before Arnold could stop her she was running down the bank toward the animal. Playfully the dog picked up the stick, turned, and disappeared into the fog bank with Louise not far behind.

"Louise, come back here." It was too late. She was already out of sight.

Arnold Spencer hurried down the embankment toward the spot he had seen Louise run into the fog. He knew she couldn't be far away, but not being able to see her made him very uncomfortable. "Louise," he called again, "don't be running around in this stuff." He disappeared into the fog after her.

A few feet farther on the fog opened up and he saw his daughter looking eagerly into more fog ahead of her. "Louise, wait right there," he called, but she just turned, waved at him, and then motioned for him to come to where she was. Almost instantly she turned and disappeared into the fog.

Arnold Spencer started to call out to her again, when it hit him. This was his recurring dream, precise in every detail. The fog, his daughter waving to him, then disappearing once again. With a new sense of urgency he rushed forward to where she had been standing.

"Louise, please, wait."

"Daddy, I'm over here."

Arnold spun around to see her standing back where he had been. She was smiling. He walked back to where she was standing, his anxiety now gone.

"I wish you wouldn't run off like that," he said, slipping his arm around her shoulders.

"I was just following Lucky, but every time I got close he'd turn and run away."

They started back up the embankment toward the car. "I don't think it was Lucky," Arnold said, "but I guess we'll never know."

They were just about to the top when Grace pointed back down the hill and shouted to them, "Arnold, Louise, look!"

Both of them turned around and looked back down the embankment. There, in a momentary clearing in the fog, a small dog that looked just like Lucky was looking up at them, tail wagging furiously. In his mouth he carried a small forked stick. For a moment they stood spellbound, just staring at the animal, then the dog turned and trotted off into the fog.

Louise and Arnold made their way to the top of the hill and the three of them were just about to get back into the car when they heard the sound they would remember the rest of their lives. Somewhere up on the interstate brakes squealed and there was the sound of tearing metal and a huge crash. A car horn locked up and there were more squeals and crashes as what would turn out to be one of the worst pileups in the state's history began to take its awful toll of lives and property.

The Spencer family stood silently in the gray world that surrounded them and listened as the sound of crash after crash slashed through gloom. They were transfixed and horrified by what they knew was happening but couldn't see because of the thick, unyielding mist.

In the somber silence that followed, Arnold, Grace, and Louise Spencer thanked their "Lucky" stars they had decided to get off the freeway and chase . . . what? Could it really have been . . . Lucky?

It was late, much later than Arnold would have liked, before they got to their hotel in Los Angeles, but under the circumstances they felt lucky to be there at all. News of the accident was on all the channels as they settled in for the night. They turned on the TV and watched in complete fascination. The infamous "Killer Fog" of the Central Valley had lived up to its reputation once again, the announcer said. Southbound traffic had been tied up for hours out of Coachella Junction, the very off ramp the Spencers had decided to take in order to check out the strange little dog.

The news reported twenty-one dead, more than thirty critically injured, and at least a hundred more with injuries that required hospital treatment. It was, in fact, the worst traffic catastrophe in the nation's history.

"If we hadn't gotten off the freeway when we did," Grace said, "we would have been right in the middle of that."

"We could've been killed," Louise added.

Arnold leaned against the back of the couch and put an arm around each of them. "We were lucky," he said.

"Lucky," Louise echoed. "You know, if it hadn't been for that dog"—she turned to look at them directly—"if it hadn't been for Lucky, we could all have been killed."

Arnold Spencer was a logical man. It was true, he had seen a dog that looked amazingly like his, but his dog was locked up in a kennel two hundred miles from the accident. "Look," he said, "I will be forever grateful to whatever little mutt that was that coaxed us off the road but—"

"I know you think it's impossible," Louise interrupted, "but I'm telling you that dog was Lucky. You saw him yourself." She turned to her mother. "You saw him, too, didn't you, Mom?"

"I know, sweetheart," Arnold told her patiently, "but I called the vet. She said Lucky was still locked in his kennel. He's been there all day."

Louise Spencer leaned against her father's chest. "He saved us," she said stubbornly. "It was Lucky and he saved us. I know what I saw."

Arnold decided to let it drop. They were alive, that was the important thing. Still, there was that business with his dream. It had come true, literally. He wondered how that might fit into all of this. And there was one other thing that had him puzzled: the strength of his daughter's conviction. As he held her close and stroked her dark hair he had to admit her reaction to all of this was both surprising and very uncharacteristic.

On the trip home thoughts of their brush with death continued to occupy the Spencer family. For some reason it seemed to bind them closer together than they had been for a long time. They each held their own thoughts about the event but the mystery of the little dog that had saved them continued to stay on their minds.

Once back home they couldn't wait to get to the vet and retrieve Lucky. And Lucky was just as eager to see them. As soon as the vet opened the gate on the kennel, Lucky came bounding out to greet them. This time it was Louise who knelt down to pick up the little dog.

"Come on, Lucky," she whispered in his ear, "it's time to go home."

Suddenly Lucky jumped out of her arms and darted back into the kennel. In a moment he came back carrying a small forked stick in his mouth.

Louise gathered him up again and turned to her father triumphantly. "Look," she said, "it's the same stick."

Now it was the veterinarian's turn to be surprised. "We don't give them sticks to play with," she said, going over to inspect the kennel. "I'm sure that wasn't in there when I put him in."

Louise just ignored them all and walked out the door with Lucky cuddled in her arms. For her the matter was settled. "You did it, didn't you?" she said to the dog. "It was you. I know it was."

Grace and Arnold didn't bother to explain her strange behavior to the vet, though the mystery was now solved for them too.

Another problem that had been concerning these modern suburban parents appeared to be solved as well. Louise, for reasons neither of them quite understood, seemed to forget all about what labels were on her blouses and shoes, or whether or not any of the other girls liked her friend Ruthie. Louise, they decided, had found, in the reality of a miracle, an understanding of what was really worthwhile in life.

Arnold and Grace Spencer aren't quite sure which miracle they're most thankful for.

You and I, of course, have rational senses that tell us that an old dog of questionable worth can't possibly be in two places at the same time. But then those same rational senses tell us that dreams have nothing to do with the future. Maybe we should consider for a moment the idea that there might be other senses that connect all of us in marvelous ways we can hardly imagine.

CHAPTER 9

DADDY, COME HOME

≈≈≈

MOST OF US HAVE HAD THE EXPERIENCE OF GETTING "STUCK" IN A moment from the past. For some it's a pleasant experience, a recollection we like to replay over and over again. Sometimes it's a remembrance we'd just as soon forget but somehow can't let go of.

For ex-soldier Tommy Ellis, finding the light at the end of the tunnel was going to take a miracle.

In the final weeks of the Vietnam war the fighting closed in on Saigon itself. American forces were being withdrawn as quickly as possible, but those whose job it was to protect that withdrawal saw some of the heaviest fighting of the war. It was even more difficult because these men knew if they could just stay alive a few more days, maybe even hours, they would be out of this hellish nightmare and on their way back home.

Tommy Ellis and his buddy John had fought together side by side across half of Vietnam. Now they were part of the force protecting the final withdrawal from Saigon and they had sworn to protect each other no matter what.

It is a slice of memory from one of those last bitter hours that invades the sleep of Tommy Ellis and, night after night, pulls him screaming into consciousness.

It is always the same. The confusion of everyone running and cursing as they hear the incoming mortar rounds. Tommy and John dive for cover as the round explodes. They both wind up in the same shallow hole and as the smoke clears he is aware that his friend isn't moving. Sniper fire begins splattering all around him as he hoists John to his shoulder and races across the open ground to the only cover he can see, a large fallen tree.

Tommy screams for a medic as he gently places his friend on the ground, cradling his head and shoulders against his breast.

"You hang on, Johnny boy," he pleads, "you hear me? You hang on."

In the tortured silence between gunshots Tommy tries to coax some sound from his friend's lips. Instead John slowly grasps a small chain around his neck and pulls it loose. With his last ounce of strength he hands the chain to Tommy. He takes it without looking at the small silver medal that dangles from the chain. John slumps against his chest, his body drained of life.

"Noooooo!" The scream erupts from the depth of his nightmare and Tommy sits up in bed, staring into the dark.

Instantly he knows that he is home in his own bed, but that doesn't relieve the anguished, rapid breathing or the cold sweat that covers his chest and neck. Automatically he looks over at his wife, Colleen, who has been awakened like this for God knows how many times since their marriage.

"Did I wake you again?" he asked apologetically.

"Yeah," she replied sleepily, "as usual."

"Sorry," he said, lying back in the dark.

"It's okay," she whispered sympathetically, "I understand."

"I wish I did," Tommy said to himself, "I wish I did."

The years since the war had passed, but not the memories. Etched like scars in the recesses of his brain, they were always there. Memories of the blood and pain and destruction. Memories of John, who had died in his arms. Memories of wanting desperately to save his buddy's life, and of his failure to do so. Memories: constant, recurring, relentless, and always painful.

As usual, Tommy was the last one up. Colleen was already dressed in a smart business suit by the time he walked into the kitchen.

"There's toast on the table," she said, "and the coffee is fresh. Do you want some cereal?"

"No, this is fine," he said, taking a cup from the cupboard and filling it with coffee. "What's with the outfit?"

"I've got a job interview today, remember?"

"Oh, yeah," Tommy replied without much enthusiasm. "I wish you wouldn't do that." Tommy sat down at the table and picked up one of the pieces of toast. "We agreed it was more important for you to be here for Ellen."

Colleen turned and looked at him, and her resolve began to melt in the helplessness of his gaze. For eighteen years they had struggled to try and hold to their original plan. Tommy would make a living, Colleen would make a home for their children. The fact that there was only the one daughter was not the only sacrifice they had been required to make.

"You know I'd rather be here when Ellen comes home from school, but, Tommy, we've got to do something."

"Right." Tommy took another sip of his coffee and stared into the cup. "I'm working on it, you know," he reminded her without looking up. "I'll find something."

"I know," she said softly, and began to clear away the dishes. It always tore at her heart to see him looking so defeated, but, she reminded herself, she had to do something.

"Morning, Daddy."

Their seventeen-year-old daughter, Ellen, bounced into the room.

"Hi, sweetheart," Tommy looked up and smiled. "How's my darling daughter?" If there was one bright spot in his life it had just entered like a ray of sunshine.

"I'm fine. Got a test today, but I'm ready." Ellen looked over at her mother. "Hey, you look fantastic. What's up?"

"Job interview."

"Oh, yeah, I remember." The sudden silence reminded her that she had touched on a very ticklish subject with her parents and one she wished would go away. She had tried to convince her father she was perfectly capable of taking care of herself, which, of course, she was. What she didn't realize was that the difficulty now went much deeper than that, and it was all caught up in Tommy's lack of self-esteem and his definition of what it meant to be a man.

"Uhhh, look," Tommy said, standing up and starting for the door, "I've got a couple of leads to follow up myself today, so if I'm not here when you get back don't worry about it." He ducked out, leaving Colleen and Ellen alone, trying to understand but finding it more and more difficult all the time.

Tommy Ellis tried to be a good worker, but he was restless and had trouble remaining focused on a job. Changing employment was at the very least a yearly event and the periodic stretches without a steady paycheck created understandable stresses in what otherwise was a very solid marriage. It was, all of them knew, a nagging remnant of his experience in Vietnam, and no one in the family escaped its effect.

"I'll see you later, hon," Colleen, said, kissing Ellen on the cheek. "Try not to worry."

"Sure, Mom."

After her mother left, Ellen walked back toward her parents' bedroom. Tommy was busy getting dressed to go out.

"Are you and Mom going to be okay?" she asked.

Tommy went about tucking in his shirttail and avoided looking at her. "You know how it is," he said, trying to be as nonchalant as possible. "We'll get through this. I'll find a job. Always do, right?" She didn't answer, so he glanced in her direction. "Right?" he repeated.

"You had your dream again last night, didn't you?"

It was a familiar question and Tommy just shrugged. "Did I wake you up too?" he asked.

"Oh, not really. I just . . ." She looked steadily at her father. "It's a stupid dream," she said angrily. "I just wish it would go away."

"Yeah," Tommy said, turning to face her, "me too."

As much as Tommy wanted and desperately needed a way out of his difficulties, the answers seemed out of reach. How could he ever find a way to escape the past? And now an interesting thing was happening, something he hadn't mentioned to Colleen or even fully come to grips with himself. The dream seemed to be getting longer. Each time it came back there was more detail, more of what had happened before the mortar round struck, bits and pieces of other things that happened after.

It was maybe a week later when the dream came again. This time he saw John rushing toward his foxhole, running bent over, low to the ground to make as small a target as possible. An instant later he dived into Tommy's foxhole, a huge grin on his face.

"Tommy," he shouted, "we're going home."

"What . . . who?"

"Everybody, man, the whole outfit. We're going home, you hear me? Home!"

Without thinking they both stood up and began to dance around when suddenly they heard the scream of the incoming rounds. Both of them dived back into the small foxhole as the explosion threw up mud and debris and shook the ground like an earthquake. From that point on everything was the same, scene by anguished scene, until John reached up and pulled the chain from his neck. Here again there was a glimpse of something just a little different. It seemed that John was trying to pull himself up, trying to say something. Tommy couldn't hear anything but his own voice: "I got to get you to a medic. You're going to be okay, I promise," but the end was always the same. John slumped against his chest and Tommy was powerless to do anything but scream for a medic and scream at his helplessness against this specter of death.

In reality this event had been something of a miracle by itself. Tommy had survived a direct hit, virtually without a scratch. Now it seemed that very fact was destroying him. Somehow Tommy believed that the mortar shell that took the life of his best friend had really been meant for him. That thought had haunted him now for nearly twenty years and only a miracle would set him free.

The following week Tommy got some important news. He had been offered a job, a good job. There was just one hitch.

"Kansas City?" Colleen was happy and sad at the same time. "And you told them you'd take it?"

"It's my first offer in a long time, Colleen, and it's a good offer. This could solve a lot of problems."

"But what about us? I've just started a job here." She was trying to be understanding, but the implications of what he was suggesting overwhelmed her.

"I know, but if this works out," he said defensively, "you wouldn't have to work."

Colleen threw her hands up in exasperation. "Tommy," she said evenly, "even if that's true, it would be next to impossible to sell our house right now—and what about Ellen? Don't you think it would be unfair to pull her out of school so far into her senior year?"

Tommy knew that what she was saying was true, but he was a man at the edge of survival. "If I don't take this job," he said, desperately, "what'll I do?"

The question brought the discussion to a sudden halt. Colleen recognized that there was more at stake here than just a job, but there had been too many promises, too many wasted opportunities. She just couldn't take the chance.

"Maybe," she said, hesitating to let the words out, "maybe what we both need is some time apart." She dropped her head and stared at her hands, not wanting to see the expression on his face. "Maybe you should take the job."

Ellen had been studying in the next room but quickly gave her attention to what was happening with her mom and dad as the intensity of their discussion picked up. She heard her mother's suggestion and her feelings suddenly stuck in her throat. Surely she didn't mean it. Surely she didn't want the family to break up.

In that sad and desperate moment it seemed that the opportunity for any miracle that might keep this family together had surely passed. But then, miracles only work when the time and place are right, and no one can be sure exactly when or where that is.

A few days later the arrangements had been made and Tommy was packed and ready to leave. He and Colleen had said their good-byes earlier that morning, before she left for work. Ellen had gone to school early for a drill-team practice and Tommy had missed her. He had decided to wait until she came home from school before leaving. There was a special bond between this father and daughter that wouldn't let him say his good-byes secondhand.

"You be good," he told Ellen, kissing her on the cheek. "Listen to your mom, hear? And write to your old man once in a while." He gave her a big hug. "Better yet, call me."

"Do you guys really have to do this?" Ellen cried as he let her go. "Do you really have to move there?" Her voice shook and her eyes were moist with tears.

"I know it's tough," he said, taking her in his arms and fighting back tears of his own, "but we're all doing the best we can. I know it hurts." He wiped his eyes. "Believe me, I know."

He took her into his arms once again, and as they parted she tapped the small silver medal he always wore around his neck, the medal John had given him that fateful night in Vietnam.

Tommy looked into her eyes, and on a sudden impulse removed the chain from around his neck. "Here," he said, handing it to Ellen, "you've been fascinated by this since you were a baby. Take it."

"But that's—"

"I know what it is. It was John's, then it was mine, and now it's yours"—he held it out to her—"if you want it?"

"Yes," she said, fighting back what was about to become a flood of tears, "I want it very much."

Months passed and life, such as it was, continued for the Ellis family. Tommy's reports were upbeat but things weren't quite solid enough, he told Colleen, to ask them to move just yet. Then his letters stopped altogether and his phone calls became more and more infrequent.

It was getting close to graduation day and Ellen was determined to persuade her father to come home for that, even if he could only stay a day or two. Her letters the past few weeks had gone unanswered, so she had called him on the phone. He would make it if he possibly could, he had told her, but the event was almost upon them and he still hadn't given her a firm answer. What was worse, the last couple of times she had tried to call there had been no answer.

Colleen came home from work to find Ellen on the phone, not a terribly surprising place for a teenage girl to be, but Colleen noticed she didn't appear to be saying anything.

"What's up?" she asked casually.

"Trying Dad again." Slowly she hung up the receiver. "No answer now for two days." She looked up at her mother anxiously. "Mom, something's wrong. I know it."

Colleen sat down next to her daughter and took hold of her hand. "Ellen," she said, "if he could make it for your graduation we would have heard from him by now. He probably turned off the phone so he wouldn't have to tell you he wasn't coming." Colleen didn't have the heart to share her darkest fears.

Ellen stood up and walked over to the window. She stared into the street as if watching for him would somehow make him appear.

"I know you miss him," Colleen continued, "but you can't worry yourself. I did that for a lot of years and it never made any difference. I wish it had."

Ellen turned to face her mother. "You still love Daddy, don't you?" she demanded.

"Yes, I do," was the quick reply, "but I don't know how to solve his problems for him. I've tried. Nothing I ever did seemed to help." She reached out to her daughter.

Ellen looked at her mother intently. She believed what she said, and she believed passionately that their family should be together. Slowly she turned and went into her room. Colleen could identify with her loneliness and pain but knew she couldn't do anything about it.

Alone in her room Ellen's only thoughts were of her father. More than anything she wanted her family reunited. She had grown desperately worried about her father and she had an unshakable feeling that something was wrong, terribly wrong. She felt a deep and extremely urgent need to see him.

A few hundred miles away in a small, run-down apartment in Kansas City, Tommy Ellis was sitting alone at a chipped steel-and-Formica table. There were no pictures on the wall, no colorful curtains to break up the glare of the unshaded light on dirty white walls. The stark surroundings seemed to emulate the emptiness that Tommy Ellis felt inside.

On the table in front of him was the want-ad section of an old newspaper and a .38 caliber revolver. He had once again lost his job and the huge black X's drawn through some of the ads were mute testimony to the futility of his continuing efforts to find another job.

He was afraid to tell Colleen and Ellen, but the job that had brought him to Kansas City had, like all the others, evaporated in the mist of his never-ending dream.

Slowly he picked up the gun and turned it over in his hands. The cool metal felt familiar and there was a certain comfort in knowing that he could at least make one decision that would end the tortured dream forever.

Back in her room Ellen felt a sense of terror grip her heart. She clutched the small medallion her father had given her and closed her eyes, trying to see him, to imagine what he was doing that very instant.

In the bleak apartment in Kansas City, Tommy Ellis was distracted momentarily by a sudden flicker of light, as if the bulb had burned out. He looked up and there, standing in the doorway, was Ellen, the medal still held tightly in her hand.

At first all he could do was stare at her in stunned surprise. Finally he found his tongue.

"Ellen . . . how did you get—"

"Daddy, I miss you so much." All the pain and loneliness of the past months was in her voice. "And Mom misses you too. She really does."

"I—I—" Tommy stammered, "I miss both of you."

"Please, Daddy, won't you come home?" she pleaded.

The surprise was beginning to slip away, replaced by the old feelings of frustration. "Things wouldn't be any easier," he said.

"But you always taught me that things worth doing aren't necessarily easy." Ellen was not going to let go.

Tommy Ellis was having a difficult time clinging to reality. The supplication in his daughter's voice tore at him. Suddenly the weight of the pistol in his hand reminded him of his earlier intent. "You're probably better off without me," he snapped.

If Ellen saw the gun she gave no hint of it as she continued to plead with her father. "You've tortured yourself all these years," she cried, "because you couldn't save John in Vietnam. But there are three other people you can still save—Mom and you and me." She held her hand out to him, the hand in which she held John's silver medallion. "Daddy," she begged, "come home. I need you."

Tommy looked at the silver medallion glittering in the harsh light. He looked into the face of his daughter and slowly extended his hand.

"Think about John," Ellen said, as their fingers touched. "Think about what he'd want you to do. Listen to me, Daddy . . . what would John want you to do?"

As the silver medallion and chain dropped into his hand the image of Vietnam exploded in his mind once again. Their joy at finding out they were going home, the shattering blast of the mortar round, John's weight on his shoulder as he ran through the rifle fire trying to get him to safety and a medic, and at last, his friend reaching up to take the chain from his neck.

But this time the ending was different. This time he remembered

John pulling his face down close to his own so he could hear the faint whisper.

"I'm not going to make it, Tommy, I know that." Tommy tried to pull away, but John held him fast. "I want you to have this," he murmured, as he dropped the medallion into Tommy's hand, "because I want you to always remember how grateful I was that you brought me in, so that I could go home to my family." Tears filled his eyes and rushed down his cheeks as he remembered John's last words: "Family, Tommy . . . family is everything."

The images disappeared as suddenly as they had come, leaving Tommy on his knees, racked with sobs. It hadn't been his fault. John knew that, had even thanked him for not having left him on the battlefield.

John didn't blame him for any of it, but in the straitjacket of guilt Tommy had fashioned for himself, John's final words had been blotted out.

At last Tommy looked up. "Ellen," he said . . . but she was gone.

It only took a few seconds to check every corner of the small apartment. She simply wasn't there. Frantically he grabbed the phone, then remembered he had disconnected it. He fumbled with the plug until he got a dial tone and punched in his number at home.

Colleen was sitting in front of the TV, not really watching anything, when the phone rang. Hearing Tommy's voice brought a quick reaction. She came up out of her chair as if she had been activated by a giant spring.

"Tommy, what . . . But I . . . No. . . ."

He wasn't giving her a chance to say much of anything and Colleen wasn't making a whole lot of sense out of what she was hearing.

"No, Tommy. . . . Ellen's here. She's in her room, I'm sure of it."

In the earpiece Colleen could hear an excitement in Tommy's voice she hadn't heard in years. "I'm telling you," he said, "it was just like she was here."

"I'm sure," Colleen replied, trying to calm things down, "that you were just missing her."

"No," Tommy insisted, "it was more than that. . . ."

At that moment Ellen came bursting into the kitchen. "Mom," she said, "it was so strange, I was sitting in my room—"

Colleen spun around and held up her hand for her to be quiet. "It's your father," she whispered, then into the phone she said, "Tommy, she's here now. She just came in."

Ellen grabbed the phone eagerly from her mother's hand. "Daddy," she cried, "are you all right? Are you coming home?"

"I'm all right now, sweetheart. Truth is, I feel better than I have in years."

"Daddy, you're not going to believe this but—"

"Yes, Ellen," he interrupted, "I believe you. In fact, I'm way ahead of you. Tell me, are you missing something? Something from around your neck?"

Ellen instinctively brought her hand up to her throat. Surprised, she looked into the puzzled expression on her mother's face and gasped. "It's gone."

"I know." Her father's voice brought her back to the phone. "It's right here in my hand."

"I *was* there," she whispered, "I really was. Oh, Daddy, I miss you so much."

"Ellen," Tommy said firmly, "tell your mother something for me. Tell her I'm coming home." Neither of them spoke for a moment, then Tommy repeated, "Tell her everything's fine now and I'm coming home."

Ellen tried to explain to her mother what had happened, but without much success. Colleen was certain she had just misplaced the silver chain and medallion and it would turn up any day now. Two days later, it did.

When Tommy got out of the cab in front of the house, Ellen rushed up and threw both arms around him. For a long time he stood there, returning her embrace. Colleen watched from a few feet back. There was something different about Tommy, a light behind his eyes she hadn't seen in years. Finally Ellen let him go. She turned to her mother, her eyes pleading and anxious. Tommy smiled. It was the old smile that had melted her heart when they met, and with a cry of recognition she rushed into his arms. They were together again, at long last.

As they turned to go into the house Tommy reached into his pocket, retrieved something, and handed it to Colleen. She took his hand and found herself holding the silver medallion. She looked at Ellen's beaming face and the surprise in her eyes slowly turned to understanding.

The circle was complete.

Tommy Ellis had pushed aside and forgotten the last words of his dying buddy, but a miracle of love had brought them back and they had hit home. He no longer rejected his miraculous survival in the war. Tommy finally understood that he had been given a precious gift, not only of his own life, but also of a loving family with which to share it.

Somehow a young girl and a simple medal had made a miraculous leap across time and space at just the right time and a good man was pulled back from the edge of darkness. Tommy Ellis came home to his wife and daughter. His nightmare of war never returned.

CHAPTER 10

DREAMS
COME TRUE

≈≈≈

T HERE ARE TENS OF THOUSANDS OF PEOPLE IN THIS COUNTRY WHO MOVE
from farm to orchard to vineyard, following the harvest. They are
called "braceros," a Spanish word for people who work with their
backs. Few of us, in this land of bountiful harvests, ever stop to consider the incredible amount of punishing work that goes into bringing
all of this to our tables, much less the hopes and dreams of the people
who make this vital harvest a reality. I'd like to share one of those
dreams with you. It's just a little dream, but it has enormous implications.

Luis Dos Santos and his family made their living harvesting the crops
along a route that took them through Texas, Arizona, New Mexico,
and southern California. They made their way from one crop to the
next in an old van that served as both transportation and temporary
housing.

Over the years, with a little skill and imagination, Luis had come up
with ways of making their rolling "bedroom" more comfortable. A
portable cookstove could turn any large shade tree into a kitchen for
his wife, Elena, and two poles and a sheet of canvas, attached to the
side of the van with snaps, made for a passable sun porch. An extra
battery that charged up during the day from the van's alternator provided lights at night to read or study by.

Study was important because Luis and Elena had two children, Teresa, a thin, dark-eyed little girl of ten, and Armando, an energetic
eight-year-old. Making sure they didn't fall behind in their studies was

a constant effort for the family. Actually, that's the very core of the dream I want to share with you.

Teresa's dream.

More than anything else Teresa Dos Santos loved to learn. So she didn't dream of being rich or famous. All she dreamed about was having a permanent home, with friends and relatives close by, and being able to go to the same school, day after day, with a teacher who would call her by name and open up the world to her through books and stories and maps. It wasn't a big dream, but to Teresa it was important, the most important thing in all the world. Because of the way her family made their living, traveling from the orange groves to the bean fields, to the sprawling vineyards, Teresa couldn't imagine how these things could come true; still, it was her dream.

They were on their way to the citrus groves when the letter finally caught up with them. Luis sat underneath the makeshift awning reading in the glare of the unshaded bulb.

"What news in the letter?" Elena asked, as she fussed with the cooking pots on the butane-fired camp stove.

"Ah, we're in luck," he said, more than a little sarcasm in his voice. "Just ten thousand dollars down and the old man who lives next to my brother Carlos will sell us the house. He will let us make payments for the rest."

Teresa, in her usual position just inside the sliding door of the van, failed to detect the irony in her father's comment. "Oh, papa," she said, "I could go to my own wonderful school every day."

Elena looked over at her beautiful daughter and shook her head sadly. "Ten thousand?" she moaned. "Why not ten million? It's all the same to us."

Luis set the letter aside and picked up the notice that had been posted at their last job, giving them the names and phone numbers of farmers looking for braceros. He and his wife came from simple, earthy backgrounds and had little education. It was a source of pride that Teresa was so filled with a desire to learn and that her brother, Armando, was following her example. But it was also a source of sorrow that he could not give them what they wanted.

One day a week, usually on Wednesday or Thursday, the farmer provided stopover transportation from the fields to the market. This meant the workers could do some shopping while the truck that hauled them to and from the fields every day waited. Luis and Elena always took advantage of the opportunity. It saved them from having to take all the trappings down from around the van and maybe lose their camping spot just to drive into town for groceries.

One midweek afternoon, as they returned from the fields and a stop at the market, the day's work settled heavily on their shoulders. Luis and Elena carried a bag of groceries under each arm as they trudged the last few hundred yards from where the truck had dropped them off to where their van was set up. Teresa and Armando, following along behind, were grateful for a little playtime. In the Dos Santos family everybody worked, but the children were usually given less demanding tasks, like carrying water to the workers or helping sort the bad fruit from the good.

Armando spotted a tin can and promptly gave it a healthy kick. When they got up to it again, Teresa sent it spinning down the road.

"Someday," she said to Armando, "we'll play this game in our very own yard."

"Don't talk foolish." Armando grunted, giving the can a vicious kick. "Things like that don't happen for us."

"If I believe it, it will happen," Teresa said with an air of finality.

"You are a dreamer, Teresa. You should listen to our papa."

"Armando!" It was his father calling.

"Yes, Papa."

"Come, be a good boy and help your mother with the sack."

Armando ran up to his mother's side and relieved her of one of the grocery sacks, leaving Teresa alone with the empty can. She kept it moving up the road as they got closer and closer to the van and one of her mother's delicious suppers.

Teresa was indeed a dreamer, and her spirit and optimism affected the attitude of the whole family. Sometimes even Luis found himself thinking about her dreams. And occasionally he even let himself think they might come true.

The campsite was in view when an errant kick sent the tin can spinning into the high weeds along the fence line. At first she thought of just leaving it there—after all, it was only an old empty can. On the other hand there was still enough distance between where they were and their camp to get in a couple more good kicks.

She walked along the fence line until she spotted the can and when she bent down to pick it up, there, next to the fence post, held fast by a prickly pear, was a tattered and faded picture, a dime-store portrait like the kind you get free when you buy a picture frame. Teresa picked it up and wiped it gently against her skirt, then looked at it more closely. The can was quickly forgotten as she ran to catch up with her mother. This simple, tattered picture, to all appearances found by accident, was destined to lead the lives of the Dos Santos family in an entirely new direction.

"Mama, Mama," Teresa cried, "look what I found."

Her mother took the faded picture from her hand and examined it closely. "Do you know who this is?" she asked, and without waiting for an answer told her beaming daughter, "This is Saint Teresa."

"Yes, I thought so, the saint I was named for."

"And you found it," her mother said, shifting the grocery sack to the other arm. "How nice."

"More than nice, Mama," Teresa said knowingly, "this is very good news."

Luis, Elena, and Armando were only interested in getting the van opened up and supper started, but Teresa knew that her finding the portrait of her patron saint meant something very important. Of this she was absolutely and totally convinced.

Later that night, when she would normally have been reading one of her schoolbooks, Teresa was still enjoying her find. Not until her father turned out the lights did Teresa close the wallet where she had enshrined her newfound treasure and pretend to go to sleep. The world had not yet driven from Teresa her trust and belief in praying for a miracle. The unexpected arrival of her namesake saint was all the encouragement she needed. Teresa closed her eyes and mumbled a quiet but fervent prayer.

It was hard to not know what everyone else was doing in the cramped quarters of the van, and Armando heard the whispered sounds.

"Are you praying for something else you can't have?" he asked her.

"That's my business," Teresa replied.

"You will never learn, girl."

"Yes," Teresa said brightly, "I will learn . . . at my new school."

"Enough, you two," Luis intervened. "The truck comes early to take us to the grove. Get some sleep."

That night Teresa tossed fitfully, caught up in the confusion of a strange dream. In it she saw a tall man with a red tie walk up to her father. The two men shook hands. It all seemed quite friendly. On one of the stranger's hands was a big ring and in the other he carried a large red valentine box. Suddenly she awoke with a startled little cry.

"Wha . . ." Luis sat up and flipped on a light, "Teresa, are you all right?"

"Oh, yes, Papa." She was fully awake now and remembered every detail of her dream. "I just had a wonderful dream. It was about you, Papa. You are shaking hands with a very important man. He is dressed in a fine suit. He has a red tie with little eagles on it and a gold pin, and he's wearing a big silver ring. We are all there, even Armando, and everyone is very happy." She paused for a moment. "Oh, I almost forgot, there is also something there like a big valentine."

Luis smiled to see her so excited, but he just reached over and patted her on the head. "It is a good dream, little one. Maybe I will win some chocolates."

"I would like that," Elena added sleepily, "but it's just a dream. Go back to sleep."

Armando just grunted and burrowed deeper into his sleeping bag.

Over the next several weeks Teresa had the same dream on five different occasions. Each time it was more vivid than before. The details about the man in the suit were always the same and always very specific. And oddly, in each dream there was always some kind of a valentine.

The harvest in this orange grove was drawing to a close, and the Dos Santos family was beginning to think of where they would be going next, when they were struck by calamity. Coming home one afternoon they found their camp had been vandalized and everything stolen.

The truck had dropped them off at the usual spot, leaving the Dos Santos family a hike of maybe half a mile. They were still some distance away when Luis saw that the awning was on the ground and the camp stools and table that were part of their camp were broken and strewn about.

"Oh, no," he said under his breath, and started running toward the van. Elena, Teresa, and Armando quickly followed. When they got there, their hearts fell. Their camp, their home really, was a shambles.

Luis hiked back up to the road, flagged down a motorist, and asked him to call the sheriff. In less than an hour a county deputy was surveying the damage.

"This sort of thing really gets me," the deputy said angrily, then he asked, "Do you have any idea of just how much is missing?"

"Everything," Luis replied, "—sleeping bags, blankets, camp stove, lanterns, radio"—he gestured hopelessly at the mess—"and what they didn't take they busted up."

Teresa didn't care about the sleeping bags and blankets; she was looking everywhere for her wallet. She was on the verge of tears as she approached her father. "My saint's picture," she said, "—it was in my wallet. Why did they have to take that too?"

"Keep looking," her father said, giving her a little hug, "Maybe it's somewhere in this mess."

The deputy began taking down all the information Luis could give him as they wandered through what was left of their camp. Elena and Armando began the task of cleaning up as best they could. It would be a cold night without the blankets and sleeping bags, but somehow they'd make do. It was having to buy the replacements that worried Luis. What little they could put away had to carry them through the long weeks between seasons. This would make them terribly short.

"Mama! Papa! Look, I found it."

Even in their despair Luis and Elena couldn't help but smile at Teresa's happy cry. She had found her wallet. The thieves hadn't taken it after all, and there, safely tucked away inside, was the picture of her saint.

Armando, however, was not so easily pleased. "You silly girl," he said, angrily, "look what's happened. Who cares about your stupid wallet?"

Teresa was undeterred. "I prayed to her," she said defiantly. "Everything will be fine, you'll see."

"You want to pray for something," Armando snapped, "pray to get our things back."

The deputy watched silently. He had seen it all so many times before. Those who have the least always seem to be the ones who get taken advantage of the most.

Suddenly the radio on the deputy's belt crackled to life: "This is dispatch to two thirty-one, you copy?"

The deputy lifted the hand-held radio to his mouth and answered, "This is two thirty-one, go ahead."

The entire Dos Santos family could hear the message that came out of the receiver. "They just picked up a couple of juveniles on the highway with a pickup load of household stuff. Sounds like it could be yours."

"That's a copy, dispatch, two thirty-one clear."

The deputy smiled as he looked into the unbelieving faces of the Dos Santos family. All but Teresa, that is. She was looking at Armando with a definite I-told-you-so air.

"If you like," the deputy said, gesturing toward his car, "I can give you a ride into town and you can check it out."

Teresa Dos Santos didn't know what the next turn of events would bring, but she knew in her heart, without a shadow of a doubt, that whatever happened would bring her closer to the answer to her prayer.

The deputy drove them directly to the sheriff's office, where Luis and Elena were immediately given a lengthy report to fill out. The things recovered from the teenagers definitely belonged to them, but there was all of the official rigmarole to go through before they could get it back.

Teresa and Armando were left to check out the comfort of the wooden benches in the hallway and make certain the water fountain continued to work. It was on one of these forays to the water fountain that Teresa saw him.

She had placed her wallet on the edge of the fountain while she pushed the button that brought the stream of water to her lips. As she finished, Teresa bumped the wallet and it fell to the floor. She jumped down off the step stool to retrieve it, but a man's hand got to it first. Someone, wearing a large silver ring on the third finger of his left hand, picked up the wallet and handed it to her.

"Don't lose this," she heard the man's voice say. "I'm sure it's very important."

Slowly Teresa looked up into the gentle and friendly face of one Señor Montoya. She didn't know his name yet; that would come later. What she did know was that he was tall and he was wearing a red tie with a gold stickpin and little gold eagles in the design.

"Papa," she shouted, never taking her eyes from the man, "Papa, come quick."

Armando had been watching and immediately darted into the room where his parents were still working on the form. A moment later all three of them came into the hall and walked rapidly toward Teresa and the man, who appeared to be quite surprised at the little girl's reaction.

"I'm sorry," Señor Montoya said, as the family approached, "I seem to have frightened your daughter."

"Papa," Teresa cried, pointing to Señor Montoya's tie, "look, it's the man from my dream."

Luis and Elena were taken aback by the sudden realization that what Teresa was telling them was true. Standing before them was the living embodiment of everything she had told them she had seen in her dream; everything except the valentine.

"No, no, señor," Luis replied, extending his hand, "she has had a dream and you do look very much like what she described."

"Oh, in that case, I am very flattered," Montoya said with a smile. "To be in a young girl's dream is a very special thing." He took Luis's extended hand in a firm grip and added, "I am Señor Montoya, the Mexican consul for this area. And you are . . . ?"

"I am Luis Dos Santos and this is my wife, Elena, my son, Armando, and this," he said, pointing to his daughter, "is Teresa."

"Luis Dos Santos!" Senor Montoya echoed the name as if he had just found a long-lost cousin. "Luis Dos Santos," he repeated, excitement still in his voice, "I have been looking for you for weeks. My office is this way, come . . . come."

Teresa clasped the small wallet close to her breast and followed them into the office. The string of circumstances and coincidences that had brought Luis Dos Santos and the Mexican consul in Fresno together that afternoon was beyond belief, but Teresa knew that whatever was going to happen would be very good because the best part of her dream was still to come: her father and Señor Montoya would shake hands and they would all feel very happy.

"I received this letter several weeks ago," Señor Montoya said, handing the paper to her father. "My office has been trying to locate you ever since."

The letter was from a legal firm in Mexico City. It told of the death of Ernesto Calderón, an uncle of Luis. Luis, it turned out, was the only heir to his estate and had been the subject of an extensive search. On the following day the time would expire for Luis to claim his inheritance before it reverted to the state.

Luis finished reading the letter and looked up at Señor Montoya searchingly. "This is no joke?" he asked.

"It is no joke, Luis. And see the date." Señor Montoya pointed to the bottom of the letter. "We have only until the end of business hours in Mexico City tomorrow to put forth your claim. Looks like we found you just in time."

Teresa stood off to one side and watched another piece of her dream fall into place. Her mother and father were pumping Señor Montoya's hand so hard, she was afraid for a moment it might come off.

"Teresa"—Armando laughed—"Papa is going to have money. Can you believe it, Teresa?"

Actually, Teresa had no trouble at all believing it. Wasn't it her dream? Had it not been in her prayers? Still, there was the matter of the valentine. No matter how hard she looked, Teresa could not see anything in Señor Montoya's office that looked the least little bit like a valentine.

Luis Dos Santos, an itinerant farm worker, received an inheritance of some twenty-five thousand dollars. Within a month the down payment was made on the small house next to his brother's and for the first time in many years the Dos Santos family would not be following the crops in the United States.

And Teresa? Well, she got the thing she desired above all others, a school she could tell everyone was her school. A school she could attend every day. The only thing that bothered her was that unresolved business in her dream about the valentine. Somehow Señor Montoya should have brought with him a valentine.

The answer to that riddle was provided on her first day in her new school. The principal had escorted her personally to her class and as she entered the room Teresa saw her teacher for the first time. She had a kind face with a quick, warm smile, and she was wearing a beautiful red dress.

"Children," the principal said, "we have a new student starting today. Her name is Teresa Dos Santos. Teresa, say hello to your new teacher . . . Mrs. Valentine."

The hopes, the dreams, the prayers, had all been answered. A home. A school. And now . . . a valentine.

I think you'll agree that answered prayers probably bring the sweetest bounty, for they are the result of the deepest wishes and the fondest hopes. And sometimes it takes the purest and most innocent prayers of a child, to be answered . . . with a miracle.

CHAPTER 11

THE
LITTLE
BLUE ANGEL

≈≈≈

THE STREETS OF MOST MODERN AMERICAN CITIES ARE BUSY, NOISY, crowded, and far too often dangerous. The workers and shoppers come in the morning and go home before dark. It is then that the streets of the city become home to the homeless, those discards of society who have slipped through the cracks. Out of luck and sometimes out of hope, they rarely see beyond the level of survival.

For nearly forty years of her life and twenty-three years of marriage, Rose Ward, quiet and unassuming, was much more than just a faceless statistic. She had a husband, a home, and all of the things that make life meaningful. With her husband's sudden death everything just disappeared and she was left in a world without money, family, or the means of support. Everything was simply gone.

Now, four years later, Rose Ward's life was reduced to existence at its most basic. She had become what is known today as a "bag lady." Her waking hours were nothing more than a daily, dreary search for food and shelter.

What Rose didn't know, and what she was about to learn, was that sometimes it's at the bottom of the barrel where the best miracles are found.

Rose had become adept at taking care of herself. Over the years she had identified certain Dumpsters and certain hours of the day when she could reasonably expect to find something that would keep her going. Her routine, toward the end of the day, took her down an alley behind a small family-owned market. Rose knew she could almost always find enough "perfectly good" food to get her through the night.

≈ **123**

The Dumpster at the end of this particular alley had become her "supermarket."

She had just gotten the heavy lid up and out of the way when a slight movement back in the alley caught her attention. Slowly she turned and squinted into the shadows, trying to get a better look. All she could see, dimly outlined against daylight at the other end of the alley, was what appeared to be the silhouette of a young girl. Rose rubbed her eyes and looked again. The shadow was gone.

It was perplexing for a moment, but since it didn't have anything to do with whether or not she got something to eat or provide warmth to the place she would sleep that night, Rose quickly put it out of her mind.

Later that afternoon, as Rose was pushing her battered shopping cart through the park, she heard someone calling her name. Surprised, she stopped and turned around.

Edith Ansela, a concerned social worker, knew Rose's background very well. She had been trying for years to get Rose off the streets, but to no avail. Rose was indigent but she was also too young to qualify for most social programs.

"Rose, I haven't seen you in a while," Edith said, as she quickly caught up to her. "How are you? Are you getting along all right?"

"I'm getting by," Rose replied tersely. She gripped the handle of the shopping cart and started it moving once again across the park.

"I've been worried about you," Edith continued, staying in step with her. "The kitchens tell me you don't come around. Have you been eating?"

Rose passed the question off with a shrug.

"There's a new kitchen just off central," Edith added. "It's in the neighborhood. Why don't you go over there?"

Edith continued to talk and Rose continued to walk, but she gave the social worker no hint that she would do as she suggested. Some people find it easier to bear their burdens alone. Rose was one of them. It was, strange as it may sound, a matter of pride. Her life, totally sheltered by a devoted husband, had left her unprepared to take care of herself when he died. And nothing in her life gave her the capacity to accept charity.

"Please, Rose," Edith said, handing her a small card, "try to stop by there. The food is quite good."

Rose took the card and slipped it into her pocket with a nod and continued on her way.

"Take care of yourself," Edith called after her. "I'll try to see you soon."

More than anything this shy, somewhat timid woman was lonely. The only family she had ever known, her loving mother, who had died when she was quite young, and her longtime husband, were both gone from this world and Rose Ward was very, very much alone.

Rose had turned the shopping cart to the right and was starting slowly along the edge of the park when she caught a glimpse of something out of the corner of her eye. She looked over her shoulder and saw, standing in a small grove of trees, a little girl with long blond ringlets, all dressed up in a blue pinafore. The little girl was looking directly at Rose and shaking her head sadly.

Could that be the same little girl I saw in the alley? Rose wondered, but she turned her head for a moment and the child was gone.

Later that night Rose was just settling down in an old warehouse she had discovered some months before. It had been gutted and the exterior was falling apart, but Rose had found a spot where the roof didn't leak and she had managed to sneak in some big cardboard boxes and an old blanket someone had thrown away. Laid on top of a pile of newspapers it made a passable bed.

Rose had two candles she kept near her bed and one old quilt she had managed to hang on to. The quilt she kept rolled up in the bottom of her shopping cart, just in case somebody discovered her bed while she was away during the day. She had just unrolled the quilt and was beginning to settle in for another cold and lonely night when she looked up and saw the same little girl again. In the flickering light of her candles the child's face literally shone and Rose could see she looked very sad.

There was no reason for her to fear a little child, but her years on the street had made her fearful of anything and everything. "Who are you?" Rose asked anxiously. "Why have you been following me?"

The little girl in the blue pinafore walked a few steps closer. "I've come to help you find something," she said, and Rose thought she saw the merest hint of a smile.

"Find what?"

"It's a secret."

"I haven't lost anything," Rose insisted.

"Of course you have, Rose. And I will show you where to find it."

"How do you know my name?" Rose pulled the quilt up closer around her. "Are you *real*? Or have I slept too many nights in this cold room?"

"I'm real enough to be here and talk to you, Rose." There was not a hint of a threat in the little girl's tone.

Still Rose wasn't satisfied. "What are you," she asked, "—my imagination? Some fairy? Or a little blue angel?"

The little girl smiled at Rose, then gave her a warm but serious look. "You go to bed now, Rose," she said softly. "Tomorrow listen for me and I will guide you where to look."

"You're not real," Rose cried. "I don't have to believe you."

The little girl put her hands on her hips and stared at Rose impatiently. Finally she removed one of two large blue bows that she wore in her hair and put it at Rose's feet.

"That's a waste of time," Rose, exclaimed. "It won't be there in the morning, I know it won't."

The little girl gave Rose another of her enigmatic smiles and retreated into the darkness. "Good night, little Rose," she said as her image quietly disappeared.

It was a while later before Rose actually drifted off to sleep. She was almost sure it was her loneliness, her isolation, and her long years on the street that were conspiring to create this delusion. Her fear really had nothing to do with the image of the little girl, it was fear that perhaps she was losing her mind.

The next morning Rose awoke with a start. The memory of her conversation with the little girl in the blue pinafore the night before was still fresh in her mind. She sat up quickly and looked at the spot where the little girl had placed the bow. It was still there. Slowly she reached down and picked it up. It was real, very real . . . and very blue.

Carefully she slipped the bow into the pocket of her old coat, rolled up her precious quilt and put it into her shopping cart, and started on her daily rounds. But today was different. Today she seemed to be going someplace in particular. True, she didn't know where that was, but she felt a definite sense of purpose as she made her way through the early-morning streets of the city.

A short time later Rose found herself standing in front of a small secondhand store. She glanced in the window for no particular reason and started to move on, but something told her to go back. Still not quite sure what was happening to her, she obeyed the impulse and turned around to see if there was something she had missed, a message, a voice perhaps.

As she stood on the sidewalk, gazing at the unimposing entrance to the secondhand shop, her hand dropped into her pocket and she unintentionally withdrew the bow. Almost instantly her attention was drawn to it.

"This?" she, muttered to herself. "This is where you want me to go?"

Rose put the bow back in her pocket and, with more purpose than she had felt for a long time, opened the door and walked into the shop.

The proprietor was an older woman, neatly dressed and very polite. "Can I help you with something?" she asked.

"I, uh . . . I was sent here," Rose replied.

The woman's response took her completely by surprise.

"Oh . . . well, they put my notice up at the community center very fast." The woman came over to her and held out her hand. "My name is Helen," she said. "I can't pay much, but there is a room in back for you to stay in. I just thought, why let it go empty if there's someone who needs a place and wants to do the job."

"Excuse me"—Rose was reeling from the implications of what she had just heard—"did you say job?"

"You do want the job, don't you?" Helen was still waiting for Rose to shake her hand.

"Yes!" Rose finally accepted the offered hand. "Yes, I want to work."

"Good," Helen said. "Come with me and I'll show you what the room looks like."

Those five words were the first genuinely positive statement Rose Ward had uttered in a very long time. "Yes, I want to work," she repeated in her mind, and was surprised at how the phrase lifted her spirits.

In just a few short weeks Rose was thriving as she helped out in the little shop. She was paid very little, but for the first time in almost four years she had a regular roof over her head, a real bed to sleep in, and, more importantly, something worthwhile to do. She had not forgotten the little girl in the blue pinafore either. The bow she had been given that night in the warehouse was placed prominently on top of the dresser in her room, and she often wondered if she would ever see the little girl again.

One evening after closing the store, while Rose was preparing for bed, she heard a strange sound coming from the shop. Immediately apprehensive, Rose called out, "Who is it? Who's there?"

There was no response, but the curtain that separated Rose's sleeping room from the shop slowly parted. In a moment the smiling face of the little girl in the blue pinafore, one large bow missing, appeared in the doorway. Rose was at once relieved and frightened.

"I shouldn't be seeing you," she said. "I know you aren't real."

"But I left you my bow," the little girl said, pointing at the bow on the dresser.

Rose looked at the bow and back at the little girl. Slowly her fears began to evaporate. "Why have you come back?" Rose wanted to know, but her tone was more gentle.

"To help you keep looking." The little girl paused, then added, "For what you lost."

"I don't know what you mean. I haven't lost anything."

"Of course you have, Rose." The little girl was quite insistent. "And when you go to the place you are needed, you will find what you lost." The little girl raised her hand and waved good-bye. "You will see tomorrow," she said confidently. "Sweet dreams, little Rose."

The little girl disappeared behind the curtain, and when Rose followed her out into the shop she was nowhere to be seen. The door, however, was still tightly double locked. These strange meetings troubled Rose a great deal, but she could sense no threat in her little friend's comings and goings and she felt strangely compelled to follow her directions.

The next day, returning from an errand for Helen, Rose walked past what had at one time been a lovely home. The architecture told her it had probably been there for many years and she couldn't help wondering what it must have been like, filled with the laughter of a happy family.

In the center of the lawn was a sign, it read: SUNRISE SENIOR RESIDENCE. Instantly Rose was drawn to it. What had the little girl said? "There is a place where you are needed."

Why this place, little blue girl? she thought. *Why have you sent me here?*

The answer might seem obvious. One of the most urgent social concerns today is senior care. And quite apart from the monetary considerations the single most difficult task of these important operations is finding sensitive and willing "care givers." But it was different with Rose. She was moved by feelings she couldn't explain; motivated by forces that, as yet, she didn't understand.

Rose Ward didn't have any formal training and certainly there was nothing in her background to recommend her, but to John Rusk, the supervisor of the Sunrise Senior Residence, Rose Ward was the answer to a prayer. The interview was brief and pleasant. When she walked out the door Rose was a full-fledged volunteer care-giver, complete with a schedule and a list of names.

Rose continued her work at the secondhand store (Helen preferred to call the merchandise "antiques"), but spent every free moment at the senior residence. There were ten residents at the home, and Rose was fond of all of them. It's fair to say they were also fond of her. Her favorite, however, was eighty-seven-year-old Mrs. Luretta Nealy. The moment they laid eyes on each other a bond was formed and Rose never missed an opportunity to be with her, to take her out into the afternoon sun for a walk, or just share long evenings of pleasant conversation.

With each passing month Luretta and Rose grew closer and closer. Rose often thought about the little blue girl, even though she hadn't seen her since her appearance at the store, and always it was with feelings of gratitude. Rose had reached out from her former painful, closed world. She was not alone anymore. Still, she wondered what the little girl had meant about finding something she had lost? There was no clear answer that came to mind.

Luretta had found a special joy in her association with Rose as well, but she knew that her time was running out. Like Rose she had been alone in the world and very lonely, but Rose had changed all that and now Luretta had some preparations to make.

Luretta called on the supervisor, John Rusk, to help her out. Specifically she asked him to make some inquiries and arrangements. Rose was not to know about it, at least not yet.

Late one evening Rose had come back to her apartment after making sure Luretta was comfortably asleep, and had decided to wash her hair. It was still wet and wrapped in a towel when she heard the familiar tingle of the bell over the front door. The store had been closed for hours and Rose always made sure it was securely locked. Cautiously she stepped out into the shop to see what was going on.

There, looking very much at home among the old four-posters and the high-backed chairs, was the little blue girl. She smiled at Rose and blew her a kiss.

"I've only come to say good-bye," she said wistfully.

"Wait," Rose pleaded, "don't go."

"I must. Now that you have found what you had lost, my job is done."

"Please, I don't know what . . ."

It was too late. Her little friend had disappeared into the darkness, but not before Rose had a chance to see that both of the bows were back in her hair. Quickly she ducked back into her apartment. The blue bow, a fixture on her dresser these past months, was gone.

Suddenly the harsh sound of the shop telephone shattered the silence. Rose rushed to pick it up before she had to listen to that awful sound again.

"Hello?" There was a long pause before Rose placed the phone gently back into its cradle. The call had brought the sad news Rose had known was coming, but dreaded just the same. Luretta was dead.

Given her age and condition it was not an unexpected message but actually hearing John Rusk say the words brought anguish to her heart. There was something between them, something special. Maybe, Rose thought, it was that undefinable something "special" the little girl had been referring to, but even as the thought crossed her mind she knew it had to be something else.

The following day Rose stopped by John Rusk's office as he had requested. She entered to find him going through a stack of papers. A cardboard box was on the desk near them. Mr. Rusk got right to the point.

"Luretta left you a small annuity," he said. "It's not large, but it's enough to keep you if you want to stop working."

"What I'd like to do," Rose replied, without a moment's hesitation, "is to become a volunteer here, full time."

John Rusk smiled. "Luretta thought you might want to do that," he said, and quickly added, "but there's something else." John picked up a file folder, opened it, and scanned the contents briefly. "Several months ago," he said, handing Rose the file, "Luretta asked me to make some very discreet inquiries for her, which I did. They concern you, Rose."

Rose took the folder and opened it on her lap. "I don't understand," she said.

"Apparently you had mentioned to Luretta that you never knew your grandparents. And she said you told her your mother's maiden name."

"Yes, that's right. It was Kinstin. My mother was born Eleanor Kinstin." Rose didn't know what was coming, but the image of the little girl suddenly jumped into her mind. *I am about to find what I had lost,* she thought, and leaned forward eagerly to hear what John had to say.

"Did Luretta tell you about her first husband?"

"Yes. Frank, I think she said his name was. Quite a tyrant, according to Luretta. He drove their daughter out of the house when she became pregnant. Luretta never saw her again."

"That man," Jack said somberly, "was Frank Kinstin. He was your maternal grandfather. Rose . . . your mother was Luretta's lost daughter."

Rose gasped, struggling to take it all in. Luretta, her beloved Luretta, had been her grandmother. Tears flooded her eyes and she longed to be with her once more, to call her grandmother instead of Luretta, to acknowledge the bond of family.

John gave her a few minutes to gather her emotions; then he reached into the box and produced an old photo album. He opened it and handed it to Rose, indicating a specific photograph.

"This is the only picture Luretta was able to keep of your mother," he said. "She was seven years old when it was taken."

Rose looked at the picture and her mouth dropped open in amazement. She touched the photograph in disbelief. It had been hand tinted but the color was still fresh. It was her little girl in blue. The blue pinafore, the ringlets, and two blue bows in her hair. Wiping away her tears Rose read the inscription beneath the photograph.

Eleanor—August 14, 1933.

Her mother had died when she was just a child. What few memories she had were warm and loving, but she had left nothing behind for Rose to cling to. Now that was all changed.

As Rose stared at the picture, her tears went away and a smile etched itself across her face. She could feel the crisp bow in her hand, hear the gentle, encouraging voice, and see the small mouth blow her a kiss. She would have those things forever.

Rose looked up at John. "Did she . . . my grandmother"—the word felt comfortable on her lips—"did she know all this . . . about me, I mean?"

"Yes, at the end."

"I really loved her." Rose looked down at the picture and sighed.

"And she loved you, Rose. She told me she loved you just as if she had known you all her life."

The reuniting of a granddaughter and grandmother, separated by a half century of heartbreak and tears, was a miracle of the first order. In the end Rose Ward understood exactly what it was that she had lost and she has been forever grateful to the little blue angel who helped her find it again. The seven-year-old girl, dressed in a blue pinafore with matching blue ribbons in her hair, had taken her lovingly by the hand and led her to a miraculous family reunion.

CHAPTER 12

A TIMELY
REUNION

≈≈≈

By the time Betty Darney reached her thirtieth birthday she had become a respected deputy sheriff in a small town in western Colorado. It was a long way from the shattered family and succession of foster homes that had been her start in life. As a young girl, statistics being what they are, not many would have given her much of a chance to make something of herself.

But here she was, single, attractive, a solid asset to her community, and totally devoted to the life she had chosen. In fact, Betty Darney seldom, if ever, thought about those early, painful years. She was far too busy with the more important matters of life, like giving a motorist a jump start when his battery died, or driving out to the Hallorans' farm with a gallon of gas so Mrs. Halloran could get into town to get her hair done.

Those were the reasons Betty loved her work: the opportunities the job provided for her to help others. She was totally caught up in it to the exclusion of just about everything else, including marriage and children. Maybe someday she would take time for those things, but not now. Besides, whether Betty realized it or not, emotional scars run deep and the pain of her own childhood was another thing buried deep in her psyche. It was a pain that she would someday have to overcome.

Early one Tuesday evening Betty was doing some household chores around her apartment when a deceptively innocent event set a miracle in motion. Betty had decided to switch blankets on her bed and when she put the one she exchanged back up on the shelf in the closet a box of old papers and photographs was dislodged and knocked to the floor.

A flood of papers slid across the carpet with one old picture coming to rest on top of the mess.

Betty had forgotten about most of the things in that box and as she knelt down to gather up the clutter she wondered why she didn't just throw all of this junk away. But when her hand reached down and picked up the photograph, some small door opened up way in the back of her mind. She gazed down at a skinny five-year-old who, at the time this photo was taken, was an abused child and a ward of the state. Tears came to her eyes as she accepted the realization that the pained little girl, with her hands behind her back, toes pointed at each other, squinting unhappily into the sun, was she.

She remembered the day the picture was taken. It was in front of her home in a small town in the Midwest. The people from the welfare department had come to take her away from a father who couldn't stop himself from beating her and a mother who couldn't stop the father. The worker had stood her next to the gate and snapped the picture.

"I'll give this to you later," she had told the frightened little girl. "Now we need it for our records."

Somewhere along the line, as Betty was being shuffled back and forth from foster home to foster home, the social worker had made good on her word. Betty had hung on to the picture for no better reason than it was one of the few things she had that was truly her own.

As she looked more closely at the photograph a semblance of a smile touched her lips. She remembered the very first couple she had been sent to live with. She could only recall their first names, Frank and Mary, but she remembered they had taken her in with happiness in their hearts and treated her with love and kindness until one day, for reasons she never understood, the authorities came and took her away. After that foster homes became a stark and brutalizing experience.

Betty lost all contact with Frank and Mary, but the memories of that one brief period of happiness in her life never left her. One thing in particular had stayed with her all these years. It was a little verse her young foster mother would say to her whenever things seemed to be going wrong. The words were simple but full of hope and faith. Betty found herself saying them now, out loud.

The clouds must burst and rain, my dear,
Before we see the rainbow clear.

"I still love rainbows, Miss Mary," she whispered to herself. And as if in response an old memory came flooding back. Mary's gentle touch and soft voice reached out across the years. She would pick Betty up, hold her on her lap, and say, "Sometimes we have to go through a storm first, to get to the things we really like. Remember, there's a flower somewhere for every raindrop. And when you see the rainbow, then everything is all better again."

Betty smiled and slipped the photograph back into the box. Funny, she thought, how a picture of such a sad moment can generate such pleasant thoughts.

Betty got up the next morning and went to work. Her well-marked vehicle was a familiar sight around town and she was kept fairly busy just returning all the friendly waves she got from her neighbors. But something interesting began to happen to Betty. Nothing very out of the ordinary, really; it's probably happened to all of us at one time or another. Usually it's a song lyric or a phrase, or even a familiar melody, that sticks in our mind and plays over and over again like a broken record. For Betty it was the remembered words of her foster mother: "The clouds must burst and rain, my dear,/Before we see the rainbow clear."

Betty tried to dismiss the recollection, but day after day went by and it seemed that with every lull in activity the lilting phrase would pop back into her mind. Sometimes, just when it seemed the phrase might disappear back into the recesses of her memory, something would happen to make it come back to the front again. Like the day she was on her way to the shopping center to give the store owner a hand in quieting down some rowdy kids. She was just pulling into the parking lot when a young boy and his mother caught her eye. In the boy's hand was a brand-new kite and on the front of it was the depiction of a bright-colored rainbow.

Even at the station house she wasn't immune. Russ, her supervisor, had been checking the duty roster with her and told her she was scheduled to be off the sixth and seventh.

"Any problem with that?" he asked.

"Don't think so," Betty replied. "Let me check the calendar." She reached over and flipped the page to the following month and there, before her, big as life, was the photograph of a beautiful rainbow.

Apparently she was staring at the picture, because Russ suddenly wanted to know if everything was all right.

"Huh? Oh, yeah, the sixth and seventh is fine," she said absentmindedly.

"Are you sure you're all right?" Russ asked again.

"Yeah, I'm fine," she said, coming back to the real world. "It's just that all of a sudden I've got this thing with rainbows. They keep popping up all around me."

"That's not so bad," Russ countered. "I have the same problem with chocolate doughnuts. Look what it's doing to my middle." He patted his ample stomach and walked away, leaving Betty with a smile and the calendar picture of a rainbow.

Betty's affinity for rainbows continued. One afternoon she pulled a motorist over for making a "rolling stop" at a stop sign. As she approached the back of the station wagon she spotted a small rainbow decal in one of the rear windows. Once again the ditty popped back into her mind: "The clouds must burst and rain my dear,/Before we see the rainbow clear."

"Officer? Officer?" The motorist brought her back to reality. "I guess I rolled through that stop back there. My mind must have been somewhere else."

Betty had the pencil poised over her ticket book, but had to smile. "Yeah," she said, "I know what you mean." She put the ticket book away. "Look," she added, "there's a lot of traffic at this intersection. Try to be a little more careful next time."

"Yes . . . I will. Thanks, officer."

The station wagon pulled away and Betty Darney stood there, watching the rainbow decal disappear.

For more than a week now it seemed like everywhere she went, everywhere she looked, there were rainbows. Big rainbows, little rainbows. About the only thing she hadn't seen was a *real* rainbow. She couldn't clear her mind of it, and now Betty was beginning to wonder if maybe it didn't have some larger meaning; though what that might be she didn't have a clue.

A couple of days later things took another unexpected turn. The wind was whipping it up pretty good on this particular afternoon, and an elderly couple traveling through Colorado in a pickup truck with a high profile camper in back decided that was a good enough reason to get off the interstate for a while. They could find a campground and maybe catch up on the laundry and do a little shopping.

Not being familiar with the town it took them a few minutes to find the local Laundromat, but they were used to the routine and before long they were pulling into the parking lot of a supermarket. The woman's sharp eyes had spotted the sign for a Laundromat just a couple of doors down from the supermarket entrance.

"Why don't I go ahead and do the laundry?" the woman said. "When I'm through we can pick up a few things at the store."

"Sounds good to me," the man replied, "but if you're gonna be a while, I think I'll just stay here and take a little nap."

The woman nodded her approval and the man eased over to the edge of the parking lot where the camper rig would be more out of the way. He turned the truck toward the Laundromat and backed into one of the marked parking stalls.

Both of them climbed out of the cab and walked around back. The man unlocked the camper door, and dropped the keys in his pocket, then helped his wife up the step into the camper. The truck rocked slightly as both of them moved around inside, but a few moments later the woman came out with a couple of plastic bags of dirty clothes and the camper settled into place. Inside the old man lifted himself up onto the bed that was permanently made up over the cab, stretched out with a contented sigh, and drifted off to sleep.

Out in the parking lot the wind continued to blow things around, and one of the things it picked up was a cardboard box somebody had stuffed with paper and lost, probably out of the back of a pickup. The wind bounced it around among the parked cars, then slid it along the asphalt toward the back of the parking lot. A sudden gust caught it just as it was about to disappear between two parked cars, and instead whipped it up underneath the old couple's truck and camper, where it lodged firmly against the tailpipe. The truck had been on the road most of the day, and the tailpipe was still hot. Cardboard has a very low kindling temperature. It was only a matter of minutes before the edge of the box began to glow a bright red and send up a curl of white smoke.

At two-thirty P.M. Betty was scheduled to pick up some paperwork at the courthouse. Although she knew the way blindfolded, she had inexplicably taken a wrong turn. Perhaps her mind was somewhere else, on another rainbow maybe; but whatever the cause, it only took her a minute or two to realize she was going the wrong way. She smacked the steering wheel in frustration and pulled over to the side of the road to let the traffic clear so she could turn around. As she looked back over her shoulder, two things caught her eye almost simultaneously: the sign on the Laundromat, which said RAINBOW LAUNDRY CENTER, and the white smoke and flames, now pouring out from under the truck and camper in the parking lot.

Betty slammed her vehicle into first gear and peeled into the parking lot. In seconds she was at the rear of the camper, pounding on the door and shouting at anyone who might be in there. The door was locked.

There was no answer, but smoke was pouring in around the door and windows and she could hear someone coughing inside.

That was enough. Using her elbow she gave the glass in the camper door a sharp crack, reached in and unlocked the door from the inside, and quickly pulled it open. As she did so smoke billowed from the interior. Betty took a huge gulp of air and ducked inside. A few minutes later she appeared at the door once again, dragging the old man and shouting at one of the bystanders to give her a hand.

The woman was just getting ready to start her second batch of clothes when she noticed people running across the parking lot. Peering through the window, she saw the truck and camper in a cloud of smoke and rushed out the door of the Laundromat, her heart pounding. She arrived just in time to see Betty lay her husband on the ground. He was gasping for breath but was otherwise okay.

The old woman knelt beside him and took his head in her hands, trying to wipe away the smoke and grime. Gratefully she turned to Betty.

"Thank you," she said. "I don't know what happened here, but thank you."

By now Betty had spotted the source of the smoke and kicked the still smoldering box of paper away from the undercarriage of the truck.

"Looks like that box got caught up against your tailpipe," Betty said. "I'm sure your husband will be all right, but why don't I take you over to the hospital just in case?"

They helped the old man to his feet and Betty drove them to the hospital emergency room and made sure they were all checked in.

"I'll see to your camper," she told the woman as she turned to leave, "and I'll stop by tomorrow just to make sure he's okay."

"Thanks again, Miss . . ." but Betty was gone before the woman could get her name.

The wind had brought with it a cold, drizzling rain, and by the time Betty got to the hospital the next day the town was pretty well soaked. The hospital had decided to keep the man overnight for tests and observations. He had gotten a pretty good dose of smoke before Betty dragged him out into the open, and they wanted to make sure there wouldn't be any residual effects.

As Betty walked in, the woman was sitting next to the bed, watching the rain splash against the window.

"Hello again," Betty said brightly.

The woman looked up and smiled. "This is the officer that saved you," she said, nudging her husband gently.

The man started to sit up, but a coughing spell made him realize that probably wasn't a good idea.

"The nurse tells me," Betty continued, "that you're much better today."

"Yeah," the man replied, "just a little too much smoke in my lungs."

"He's doing just fine," the woman added, "thanks to you."

"We're just lucky I happened by when I did," Betty told them. "That's not a street I'm usually on."

The old man turned to his wife. "Well, like you say," he whispered, "there's usually a reason for these things."

"Just another storm for us to weather, that's all," she said, patting his hand. And then to Betty's amazement she heard the woman say, "The clouds must burst and rain, my dear . . ."

Betty finished the ditty: "Before we see the rainbow clear."

The old woman looked at Betty in surprise. She had invented that little rhyme. Hardly anyone knew of it.

"I didn't get your names yesterday," Betty asked tentatively.

"My name is Frank Meyher," the man said, "and this is my wife—"

"Mary!" Betty blurted the name out before the man had a chance to finish.

The old couple looked at each other, then back at Betty.

"Yes, that's right," the woman said. "How did you know?" Slowly she stood up and walked over to Betty, her eyes drawn to the small metal plate with her name on it.

"Darney," she said quizzically. Suddenly Mary brought her hand to her mouth and gasped. She searched Betty's face for some sense of familiarity and slowly the recognition came. Mary turned back to her husband. "Darney," she repeated, "it's her. It's our Betty."

A lump had come to Betty's throat and tears sprang to her eyes as the full realization began to sink in. She stood stunned, motionless, unbelieving.

"Oh, my heavens," Mary cried, "oh, my heavens it is you, isn't it?"

"Yes" was the only word Betty could get out.

Mary threw her arms around her and held her tightly. "They took you from us," she said, her voice full of tears and excitement. "We tried so hard to get you back. Then you disappeared. We've been searching for you. We've missed you so."

Betty Darney let her arms enfold the only kind and loving mother she had ever known, and the two of them wept unashamedly. Frank's cheeks were wet, too, when the nurse looked in on them, but he insisted it was just the effects of the smoke. It didn't matter. Frank and Mary and Betty . . . were a family again.

CHAPTER 13

THE BOY
ON A BIKE

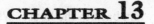

ALBERT EINSTEIN SAID: "THE MOST BEAUTIFUL THING WE CAN EXPERI-
ence is the mysterious. It is the source of all true art and science."
Certainly one of the most beautifully mysterious things we have encountered in our search for miracles and other wonders is the unexplainable link that so frequently occurs between one family member
and another. Without any rational explanation some fathers and sons,
mothers and daughters, sometimes brothers or even uncles or grandparents, develop a bond that lets them know, even though they are
separated by great distances, what the other family member is doing or
feeling. It's a powerful link that no one has been able to explain and it
seems to be there for a lifetime . . . sometimes beyond.

Nathan Sharpe was a typical teenage boy, bright, energetic, and
outgoing. He was at that wonderful age when being able just to jump
on his bike and go represented freedom and the passage from boy to
man. Nathan was already thinking about driving the family car or even
buying himself a motorcycle. His bike, in fact, frequently became a sort
of surrogate motorcycle as he visualized himself flashing down the
highway, the roar of the engine muffled only slightly by the helmet he
would be wearing, only because it made his mother feel better.

Nathan Sharpe was typical in just about every way except one: his
relationship with his grandmother.

As far back as Nathan could remember his grandmother had always
been there when he needed her. Even as a small boy, when he had
fallen from the old tree out behind his grandfather's barn, completely
out of sight of everyone, his grandmother had suddenly appeared to

comfort him and carry him back to the house. What's more, it seemed to be a two-way street. Once, while watching TV, Nathan had suddenly jumped up and run to the basement to find his grandmother crouched at the bottom of the stairs, holding her ankle. She had sprained it when the bottom step gave way.

To be sure, Nathan didn't know this was not the typical way of things. So far as he knew everyone's grandparents could tell when their grandchildren where in trouble and grandchildren knew when grandparents needed help. Furthermore, now that his grandmother was living with them, he just took it all for granted.

In fact if you were to ask him, Nathan probably would have told you his was a perfect arrangement. He had his grandmother and her marvelous chocolate-chip cookies, and he had his bike. At this moment in time he couldn't imagine life without either of them.

What the car was to his dad, the bike was to Nathan. It was his passport to adventure. Wheels! The way he got to and from almost every place. But not even Nathan could have planned on the amazing and miraculous adventure one of his bicycle rides would give him.

It was a typical Saturday morning in a typical suburban neighborhood. Nathan had just taken his bike out of the garage and walked it over to where his father, Don, was washing the car.

"Hey, nice job, Dad. Wanta wash my bike?"

His father playfully turned the hose in his direction and Nathan ducked out of the way.

"Just remember," his father said, "when you start drivin', you start washin'."

"That's okay by me," Nathan shouted as he jumped on his bike and started down the drive.

"Hey, hold it." Meredith Sharpe, his mother, was calling him and Nathan put on the brakes. "Where are you off to?"

"Just ridin' around with John."

Nathan's grandmother appeared in the doorway next to her daughter-in-law and waved at Nathan.

"Okay," his mother said, "but don't be long. We're all going to the drive-in for lunch today."

"Okay." Nathan waved to the two women. "See ya later, Grandma."

"You be careful now, ya hear?" his grandmother called, as he jumped over the curb and began pumping up to speed. A slight twinge of concern tugged at her heart as she watched him go, but she quickly put it aside.

There was more than love between Nathan and his grandmother; there was also a full measure of understanding. Friendship *and* communication on this fine fall day would usher both Nathan and his grandmother into the realm of miracles.

Just as he had a dozen times on any average day—on hundreds of days like today—Nathan rolled down the sidewalk as if he owned it. But today would turn out to be not quite so average.

A few blocks from home Nathan spotted John, waiting on the preappointed corner. With a screeching stop Nathan slid his bike up alongside his friend.

"What took you so long?" John asked, standing on his own pedals and pushing off. "I've been waitin' for ya."

Nathan quickly fell in beside him. "Why? What's up?"

"Tony's brother just got a motorcycle." John was up off the seat, pumping hard for greater speed. "Thought we should cruise by there and see if maybe we can talk him into giving us a ride."

"Cool!" Nathan shouted, and started to put more leg power into his own pedals.

"Okay. Let's hit it."

In teenage parlance that was a challenge and both boys began to exert maximum thrust.

Back at the house Nathan's mother and grandmother were having a discussion about the importance of where one stores one's cooking utensils.

"I don't know why you don't keep your baking sheets in the house," Grandma said.

"Because I only use them when you're here," Meredith replied, "and until recently that wasn't very often."

"Well, you know me," Grandma replied, "I'm not happy unless I'm baking for someone."

The only thing odd about this discussion was that it was taking place in the garage. Meredith got a small stepladder and placed it near some shelves on the garage wall. She climbed up several steps and retrieved a large plastic bag from the top shelf, then turned to hand it down to Grandmother Sharpe, who for some reason was staring down the street in the direction Nathan had gone.

Meredith climbed down the ladder and walked over to Grandma. "Well, here they are," she said, smiling. "It's up to you now."

"Wha—" Grandma Sharpe turned quickly and took the cookie sheets from her. "I'm sorry," she said. "I was distracted. I didn't even see where you got these."

"Right up there," Meredith said, pointing at the top shelf. "They have that top space all to themselves."

"Oh, my," Grandma said, caught between the strange storage place for baking sheets and the growing sense of uneasiness she was feeling, "I hope I don't have to climb up there every time I want to bake cookies." She paused and looked back down the street. "Where did Nathan say he was going?" she asked.

"To his friend's house," Meredith replied. "He won't be long, I'm sure. Probably get back just in time to sample the first batch out of the oven."

The skill and precision youngsters can bring to the relatively simple task of riding a bike can rival that of a top-gun pilot. Except of course, they lack experience and . . . any sense of caution.

The two boys, racing toward the excitement of a motorcycle ride, were only aware of each other. John, flying down the sidewalk, Nathan, slipping the curb and plunging headlong into the street, gave no thought to the possibility of danger.

Suddenly, out of nowhere, a van turned the corner and the driver looked up to see a bicycle heading right for him. The boy on the bike was looking back over his shoulder and didn't look up until it was too late for either of them to avoid the inevitable collision.

The screech of brakes that interrupted the peace of the neighborhood was followed by a sickening thud.

Several blocks away Grandma Sharpe dropped the cookie sheet she had in her hand. "Nathan!" she screamed, and ran out the door.

"Mother, what is it?" Meredith's heart was in her throat. She was aware of the bond between her son and his grandmother, and she didn't hesitate to follow her out the door, shouting at Don to join them.

Grandmother Sharpe was new to this town, but she hurtled down the street as if she were being guided by some invisible hand. Don and Meredith, hurrying to keep up, were trying to get her to tell them what was wrong.

"It's Nathan" was all she could tell them, "something has happened to Nathan."

The driver of the van was out of his vehicle the second it stopped moving. There, partially obscured by the front of the vehicle, Nathan Sharpe lay pale and unconscious.

"Someone call an ambulance," the driver shouted, *"Hurry!"* A young man broke from the crowd that had quickly gathered and ran across a lawn to one of the nearby houses.

Curious onlookers crowded in closer as the driver of the van dropped to his knees next to Nathan. The boy was very still. A small trickle of blood came from his mouth, another ran down the side of his head. Off to one side the bicycle lay, hideously twisted. Helplessly, the man turned to the crowd. There was nothing he could do. Nothing he dared do.

Moments later the scream of a siren announced the arrival of an ambulance. The crowd parted, and the machine pulled in as close to the accident as possible. Nathan would say later that he stood in the crowd and watched as the two paramedics jumped out of the ambulance and rushed to where his body was lying on the pavement.

Nathan Sharpe, through some process we don't understand, but which has been documented many times, was somehow out of his body. In silence he watched as the paramedics began their work. And for some reason he felt compelled to listen carefully to every word that passed between them.

"Pupils fixed and dilated," the first man said, gently lifting Nathan's eyelids.

"Probably shock. Let's get the legs up," the second man replied.

"I've got a lot of bleeding here," the first man reported as they turned Nathan's head carefully to one side.

"Okay, get a compress on that. Just enough pressure to stop the bleeding. There may be broken bones."

"His pulse is fading."

"If he's breathing, it's so shallow I can't read it."

"Clear the breathing passage."

The men moved swiftly and efficiently as the conversation passed back and forth. Nathan watched dispassionately. He felt nothing, but his senses were active and alert.

Suddenly there was a small commotion in the crowd as Nathan's grandmother pushed her way through, followed closely by his mother and father. He heard his mother gasp and fall to her knees by his side. He watched his father reach down and take her by the shoulders as the paramedic, gently but firmly, lifted her to her feet. And he saw the tears in his father's and his grandmother's eyes.

"What happened?" Meredith turned to her husband, then back to the paramedics. She was sobbing, barely in control of herself. "What happened to my son?"

The paramedic looked at Don. "Are you this boy's parents?" he asked.

"Yes," Don replied hoarsely, fighting his own emotions, "yes, we are."

"I don't know what happened here," the medic said compassionately, "but we're doing everything we can. Please try to stay calm." He turned back to help his partner. "C'mon," he said, "let's get him into the ambulance."

Nathan's grandmother was standing next to Meredith, trying to console her. Nathan remembered thinking how sorry he was that they all felt so bad. Then he heard a voice. He stood very still and listened as they lifted his broken body onto a stretcher and moved it toward the ambulance.

"Yes," he said, in response to the voice, "I understand. I will tell her."

As his body went into the ambulance, Nathan said he just sort of went in with it. His parents and grandmother crowded in close to the back of the vehicle in time to hear one last bit of conversation between the paramedics.

"I'm getting a good pulse now."

"His breathing's stable. Let's get him out of here."

The door closed and the ambulance sped away, sirens screaming. Nathan's parents and Grandma Sharpe stood holding each other in a tight little circle. Nothing to do now but get back to the house as quickly as possible and get over to the hospital. It was then that Don noticed John, standing next to his bicycle, his face wet with tears.

Don walked over to him and put his arms around the boy's shoulders.

"What happened, John?" he asked quietly.

John's head dropped against Don's chest as he tried to explain that they were just going to Tony's and Nathan had ridden into the street. He didn't see the van until it was too late.

Nathan's grandmother walked up and put her arms around John also. "It's all right," she said, "Nathan is going to be all right."

Don looked up at his mother. She was almost smiling. "How do you know that?" he said.

"He told me." Her voice was fully confident. "As they were putting him in the ambulance he told me not to worry, that everything was going to be fine."

"Come on, Mom," Don said, turning her toward Meredith, "let's get to the hospital."

Nathan's injuries were very severe, but in spite of that he fully recovered with only a few lasting scars. During his convalescence the doctors had marveled at how confident he was that he was going to be just fine. He was, they told his parents, much more confident than they were. Of course, the doctors didn't know that during the time he was clinically dead Nathan had heard a voice tell him he would be all right and to reassure his grandmother.

That miraculous experience should have been enough for anyone in just one lifetime, but for Nathan Sharpe it was merely the prelude to another miracle yet to come.

It was nearly a year later. Nathan and his family had put the tragedy of his accident far behind them and Nathan was once more acting like a typical teenager. Nathan's grandmother had, by now, grown comfortable around the house and around the town and was truly an integral part of their family. As far as Nathan was concerned she might even be the most important part of the family. The cookie jar was hardly ever empty and Nathan had come to rely on that for fuel the same way his father relied on the gas station.

Nathan had replaced his old bike with a brand-new "mountain bike." A five-speed shifter, front and rear pressure brakes, and heavy-duty, knobby tires, were the principal features of this vehicle. It was not designed for speed, but to go just about anyplace you could walk or hike.

He and a bunch of the guys had planned a "rough ride" for this particular Saturday morning, and Nathan let his grandmother know he was counting on her and the cookie jar to keep him alive when he got back home.

It was close to noon when John rode into the driveway. He sat waiting patiently for Nathan to get his bike out and join him. It would be fair to say that since Nathan's accident both boys had achieved a whole new level of caution. They rode easily down the street in the direction of the park.

As they disappeared around the corner, Meredith came over to Grandma Sharpe. "Don and I have to go into town for a while. Would you like to come along?" she asked.

"Oh, no," grandma replied, "I've got to get busy on another batch of chocolate chip cookies."

They both laughed. "Well," Meredith said, "you know where the cookie sheets are." Don showed up just then and she added, "If we could get somebody to build me some more cupboard space, we could keep them in the house." She punched her husband in the ribs as they walked out the door.

Nathan still loved his bike. He especially liked getting off the designated paths and running up and down the modest hills in the park. The whole group was in the middle of doing just that when Nathan suddenly slammed on the brakes and skidded to a stop. It took John completely by surprise, so it was another ten yards before he could get stopped. He turned back to see Nathan staring into the ground.

"Hey, Nathan," he called, "are you okay?"

There was no answer and John turned around and came back to where he was standing.

"Nathan?"

Nathan glanced up at his friend and whispered, "Grandma!"

Whatever caution Nathan had learned was suddenly thrown to the winds as he jammed the pedals down with all his strength and began propelling his bike across the park in a straight line toward the main entrance. John was only a moment behind him.

As they turned the last corner to his house, Nathan was pedaling with a fury. He saw that the garage door was open as he turned into the driveway, and in almost the same instant he saw his grandmother's still form lying on the floor.

The bike was still moving when he jumped off and rushed into the garage. He knelt by her side, a feeling of helplessness washing over him. She was unconscious. The broken ladder lying crazily on its side and the cookie sheets scattered across the floor told him what had happened.

As he reached toward his grandmother the helplessness suddenly vanished and a quiet calm came over him. Like instructions, the words of the paramedics who had attended him after his own accident filled his ears and he began doing what he was told.

He checked her eyes. They were fixed and dilated. Shock. He turned her carefully onto her back and grabbed a rolled-up sleeping bag off the shelf to slip under her feet to elevate her legs.

John showed up just as Nathan was preparing to move to his grandmother's left side, where he noticed a lot of bleeding.

"John," he shouted, "get in the house and call nine one one. Hurry!"

John spun on his heel and disappeared through the door.

"Quite a bit of bleeding here." The voice was very clear. "Need a compress, just enough pressure to stop the bleeding."

Nathan whipped off his jacket and tied the sleeves around a nasty cut in his grandmother's left arm. Gently he increased the pressure until the voice told him to stop.

"Can't hear her breathing, better check the airway."

Again Nathan moved to the task as if he had been doing it all his life. Opening her mouth he tilted her head back and pulled her tongue forward. There was a sharp intake of breath.

A few minutes later the ambulance pulled into the driveway and two paramedics jumped out. Grandma Sharpe was breathing easily, the bleeding had stopped, and some color was coming back to her face.

The paramedics took the situation in at a glance. They checked Grandma Sharpe carefully, and while one of the men replaced Nathan's jacket with a real compress, the other went back for the gurney.

"You do all of this yourself, son?" the medic wanted to know.

"Yes, sir," Nathan replied. "Will she be all right? She's my grandmother."

The medic helped his partner lift his grandmother onto the gurney, then turned to Nathan. "You can relax, son," he said. "Your grandmother is going to be just fine. I'd say she's a very lucky woman to have a grandson who knows so much about first aid."

Grandmother Sharpe blinked and opened her eyes. "What . . . ?" she started to say, then remembered. "Oh, dear, I guess I fell."

Nathan leaned in close to her. "You don't have to worry, Grandma," he said, "we've got you all taken care of."

The two paramedics exchanged glances and smiled. "Yeah," one of them said, *"we* sure do."

Nathan took his grandmother's hand and added, "I love you."

After they had loaded his grandmother into the ambulance, the medic closed the door and turned to Nathan. "I don't know where you learned all this, son," he said admiringly, "but you just saved this lady's life."

"I learned it from a couple of guys like you, I guess," Nathan replied with a smile. He glanced over at John, who right up to this very moment had never quite believed Nathan's story about having watched the medics work on him. John just grinned from ear to ear.

Nathan knew, of course, that something quite extraordinary had happened. The instructions he'd heard were *not* simply a remembrance of his out-of-body experience. He had heard the words actually spoken, clearly and distinctly. He had never been trained to do any of the things he did that day, but he'll tell you plainly that he has had a graduate course in miracles.

And you'll be happy to know that among the many other benefits resulting from this "cluster" of miracles, Meredith Sharpe got a new set of kitchen cupboards. All of the cooking and baking pans are now kept in the house.

PART IV

MIRACLES OF TRANSCENDENT LOVE

≈≈≈

VIRTUALLY ALL OF US, AT ONE TIME OR ANOTHER, HAVE FELT THE POWER of love in our life. Love is the foundation of every Christian principle and, so far as I know, the basis upon which all religion is founded.

But even beyond religion, the most fundamental characteristic of all human relationships is love. Without love relationships invariably fail. With it, not even time and distance can break the bond that binds one human being to another. To say that love is the most powerful emotion of which the human family is capable is to do it an injustice. Many believe it is love that gives power and meaning to everything in the universe.

The somewhat arbitrary categories we have selected for the presentations in this book aside, it should be quite clear to anyone who has read this far that the single thread that runs through all of the miracles and wonders presented here is a prevailing sense of love.

Why, then, set aside a special category to demonstrate what is so obviously a universal principle?

The answer, as you will discover in the next three chapters, is that there is a love so strong, so powerful, that it transcends all of man's perceived limitations. A love that reaches out, even from the grave, to touch the lives of those whose hearts and minds are open to its power.

CHAPTER 14

A MESSAGE
FROM BEYOND

$\approx\approx\approx$

EVERYBODY IN LEESBOROUGH KNEW ABOUT THE LOVE OF A YOUNG COUple named Robert Jentree and Janet Rule. The high school yearbook for 1982 devoted an entire page to "John Marshall High School's own homegrown 'Romeo and Juliet.' "

Janet's mother had died and her father had already welcomed Robert into the family. He was intelligent, levelheaded, ambitious, and talented. A father couldn't ask much more than that for his daughter. But more importantly, Janet's father realized that his daughter and this young man had that rare, true love that makes incredible things happen. He just didn't know how incredible.

The year Robert and Janet graduated from high school was filled with planning for their future. There was never any question in anyone's mind, least of all theirs, that the marriage ceremony would immediately follow the graduation ceremony.

The last day of school at John Marshall High was given over to the same tradition that applies at just about every other high school in America. The students are released from class and they spend the day swearing eternal friendship and signing each other's yearbooks. Robert and Janet were full of hopes and dreams as they sat under a tree near the baseball diamond and wrote their inscriptions in each other's book.

Robert finished quickly and waited patiently for Janet to complete her thought. Then they exchanged books and eagerly read the other's note.

Janet wrinkled her nose when she saw Robert's cryptic inscription. It was just six capital letters and one number. *I LV U 4 F R.*

"I don't know what it means, Robert," she said, a note of disappointment in her voice.

Robert slipped an arm around her shoulders. "Here," he said, "follow my finger." He pointed to each letter and translated. *"I . . . love . . . you. . . . for . . . ev . . . er.* See?"

Tears glistened in Janet's eyes as she leaned her head against his shoulder. Janet would remember later that they sat there in the shade of that tree for a long time, enveloped in the warmth of their love, isolated from the problems of life and the world by the simple knowledge that from this moment on nothing could ever come between them.

They were married just a few weeks after graduation, just as everyone expected, and, just as everyone expected, their son, Jeremy, was born the following year.

Jeremy was the apple of his young father's eye, and the very fact that he was there gave Robert renewed vigor and determination. Once, while doing nothing more than holding Jeremy in his arms, Janet had noticed tears in Robert's eyes.

"What's the matter?" she had asked, surprised and concerned.

"Nothing," Robert answered, "nothing is wrong. I just want you to know that I will never, ever let you and Jeremy down. I will always love and protect you, no matter what."

"Oh, is that all?" Janet smiled, taking Jeremy from his arms and cradling him in her own. "We already knew that."

Almost from the minute he was born there was an incredible bonding between Robert and Jeremy, but no one on earth could have imagined *how* close.

Like most young couples their lives were filled with struggle and sacrifice. Robert had taken a job at a local lumberyard, where his steady effort and loyalty earned him the promotions and raises that one might expect, but as one might expect, it was never quite enough.

In spite of the difficulties, they didn't complain. Robert, a talented artist and designer, had his sights on something bigger and better: a career as a commercial artist. He went to night school and scraped enough money together to buy a drafting table of his own. When he wasn't in school he was practicing the lessons he was taught there. A few local firms that supported the school by using some of the students' work had even bought a few of his ideas.

When Jeremy turned four, Robert found a small plastic desk that kind of looked like his drafting table, so he bought it for him. After that Jeremy and his father worked side by side, Robert with his pens and brushes and Jeremy with his crayons.

Robert was building quite a handsome portfolio and several times each year he would dress up in his best suit and travel to New York, where he would make the rounds of the advertising agencies and design firms. He would show them his work, listen carefully to their comments, and try to persuade them he was the artist they were looking for. Each trip, he was certain, brought him a little bit closer to his goal of being a commercial artist in a major firm. It was a lofty goal but one he was sure he could reach. He had the talent and the tenacity. All it would take was one little break. Janet as well as Robert was sure that break would come. She rested secure in the knowledge that Robert was always looking for a way to insure that she and Jeremy would never want for anything. Then fate stepped into his plans one bright spring day in 1985.

On this particular afternoon Robert had Jeremy on his shoulders, playing the horse for his son. Together they galloped down to the mailbox at the end of the drive, Jeremy hanging on to Robert's hair and ears and squealing with delight. They were almost back to the house before Robert picked out the logo of one of the advertising agencies he had visited, in the upper left-hand corner of a very businesslike envelope.

Much to Jeremy's disappointment he suddenly found himself standing on the ground while Robert tore open the envelope. He read the contents with increasing excitement. Finally he let out a war whoop that brought Janet racing to the door.

"Robert, what is it, what's happened?"

"Janet, look," he said, excitedly, handing her the letter. "These guys like my designs. They want me to come to New York for an interview."

Two days later he was in the city. The interview went well and within a few hours of his arrival he was back out at the airport, the job he had worked, planned, and prayed for now a reality.

"Welcome aboard, Robert," the senior design artist had said. "We're looking forward to a long and rewarding association with you."

It had been all Robert could do to keep from jumping up and shouting with glee right there in the office. He had managed to hold it in, but now he had to tell someone and that someone was Janet. As soon as he cleared the reservation counter Robert went to the phone.

"Janet! Baby . . . I got the job. We're on our way. Tell the birthday boy Daddy's coming home for his party right now. I'm on the plane as soon as I hang up."

On the other end of the line Janet was ecstatic, not because she looked forward to living in New York, but because she knew how much this meant to her husband. It was his dream come true.

"Oh, Robert," she cried, "that's fantastic."

"See you in a couple of hours," Robert said, and added, "I love you madly."

Robert arrived back in Leesborough full of excitement and anticipation. It was his son's fifth birthday, he had the job he had always dreamed of getting, and he had a beautiful and devoted wife. Robert Jentree considered himself the luckiest and the happiest man alive.

He hurriedly made his way to the old, beat-up Volkswagen he had been using ever since high school and drove out of the parking lot. Once on the main road Robert was only ten miles from home.

But who can know when fortune will suddenly change?

Just six miles ahead two men left a tavern and climbed into the cab of their pickup truck. Draining the last of their whiskey they tossed the empty bottle into the back and peeled out of the unpaved parking lot in a cloud of dust and rocks.

"Those two clowns are gonna kill somebody one of these days," another patron of the bar said disgustedly, as he watched them speed away. But no one really believed it, including the two drunks now careening down the highway.

The light changed and Robert proceeded into the intersection. He barely had time to look up before the pickup truck slammed into his car.

With neither malice nor forethought life was snatched from a loving and devoted husband and an irreplaceable young father. Only the tragedy and sadness remained.

Jeremy would never have his fifth birthday party, and a piece of his little heart died on that day. Something else also died in the crash with Robert, the hopes for the future of both Jeremy and Janet Jentree.

The trauma of Robert's death left Janet devastated. Day by day, almost hour by hour, Janet had to will herself back to life and its harsh realities, and the only reason she put forth the effort was for the sake of their son.

Janet moved out of the small house they had been renting and moved back in with her father. It was a necessary move, not only for financial reasons but because Janet desperately needed someone to lean on. Her father was more than willing to be that someone, but there were times he felt helpless before the huge chasm of his daughter's grief.

"It's been almost two months, Janet." Her father's words were kind but firm. "You've got to take hold, no matter how it hurts. Jeremy needs you now more than ever."

"I know, Daddy," Janet replied, her grief robbing the words of all meaning, "but I miss him . . . I miss Robert so very much."

And there the conversations would end. Jeremy would look on with saddened eyes as his mother drifted deeper into her own gloomy world.

Their financial situation did nothing to cheer her up, either, but eventually she came to the realization that she must try and do something. Her father was far from being a wealthy man and the additional burden of the two of them would be much more than he could handle.

Little by little the six thousand dollars Robert had put in savings— "to help us move when the time comes," he had told her—dwindled away. One day she looked at the bank statement and realized they were down to just $1,206.

"I don't know what I'm going to do," she told her father, "I really don't."

"Don't worry about it," her father said, putting his arms around her. "It'll all work out somehow."

The words were comforting, but Janet knew her father was deeply concerned. Then, at the very bottom of her grief and loss, the forces of a miracle began to gather.

Janet was sitting at the kitchen table poring over the bills and trying to reconcile what she owed with the number on the last line of her checking account. It was, she conceded, hopeless. They would probably lose the car too.

"Oh, Robert," she said, gazing lovingly at the picture of her husband she always kept close at hand, "my darling Robert, I need you . . . I miss you so much."

"See, Mommy!" Jeremy had been sitting at his "drafting" table while she worked and now he was holding out a piece of paper to her.

"That's nice, Jeremy," his mother said absently, and turned back to her checkbook.

Jeremy seemed disappointed that she wasn't more excited about his "work." He looked up at her, then cocked his head to one side, as if he were listening to something. Almost immediately he put the piece of paper back on his desk and started drawing again.

It's important to remember that Jeremy was barely five years old. He had never been to school and could not read or write a single letter of the alphabet. Yet he was scratching out a series of very distinct symbols.

Once again Jeremy extended the piece of paper to his mother. "Daddy told me to write them," he said firmly.

Janet stopped what she was doing and looked at her son sadly. She knew Robert's death had been hard on Jeremy too; she just didn't seem to be able to work through her own pain long enough to deal with his.

"What is it, sweetheart?" she asked, taking the paper from his hand.

"Daddy says they are for you."

"Oh, Jeremy," she said, "please, let's not talk about Daddy now."

"But Daddy says—"

"Okay, okay." Janet gave her full attention to the piece of paper Jeremy had been writing on. She expected to see a paper full of crisscross lines, circles, and other scribbles, but what she saw made her eyes open wide with wonder.

"Jeremy, this is very good, honey. Where did you learn to make letters?"

"Daddy says it's for you," he insisted one more time.

What Jeremy had written bore a strong resemblance to the shorthand taught to Robert by his art-school teacher and friend, Jack Knowles. Janet was only slightly aware of it but she remembered Robert had told her once that it was very useful in helping him take notes in class. And there was something else vaguely familiar about it, but she couldn't quite think of what.

"Dad," Janet said, getting up from the table, "come and take a look at this."

Both Janet and her father thought that Jeremy's sudden excursion into the world of letters was curious enough to follow up. Besides, Jeremy kept insisting that his daddy had told him to give the paper to his mother.

Janet called Jack Knowles at the school and asked him if they could get together. Jack had been close to Robert for many years and he quickly agreed. He was anxious to help in any way he could.

Janet and her father took Jeremy and drove over to the school that afternoon. Jack taught some of the art classes and he invited them to go into one of the classrooms so they could reproduce Jeremy's drawings on the blackboard. One by one the letters and numbers went up on the board. When he had finished writing, Jack stepped back a couple of paces to take it all in.

"Fantastic," he said. "It looks just like the shorthand Robert and I used in school." He ran his fingers from one letter to the next and shook his head. "It doesn't seem to mean anything, though, just letters and numbers in a row."

Janet looked at the first line of letters more closely. The feeling that she had seen this before was suddenly back with her, stronger than ever.

"I don't know. . . ." She hesitated a moment, then let out a sharp cry. Both hands flew to her face. "It's Robert, Daddy, look!"

Janet grabbed the chalk from Jack's hand and drew a heavy line under each one of the letters in the first line. *I . . . L . . . V . . . U . . . 2 . . . 4 . . . F . . . R.*

She turned to her father, flushed with excitement. "In the yearbook, Daddy, remember, that's what Robert wrote me, *I love you forever.* Now, see"—she turned back to the board—"there's a two—he means me and Jeremy both."

That was enough for Jack. He took the chalk from Janet and went to the second line. "Okay," he said, "let's see if we can figure this out."

The letters were grouped differently and there were more of them, but by now all doubt that Robert was somehow trying to communicate with them had fled. It was no longer a question of "if," it was a question of "what."

MD TN BK 34 ST BX 1142. There it was before them in bold letters. All they had to do was figure it out.

"I don't know," Janet said. "could *BX* mean *box*?"

"Box 1142?" Jack framed it as a question. "Did Robert have a post office box?"

"No," Janet said, shaking her head. "What about *34 . . . ST*? Could that be *Street*?" She thought about it for a minute and frowned. "But we don't have a Thirty-fourth Street anywhere in town."

Jack turned his attention to another group of letters. "What could *BK* mean? *Bank,* maybe." He wrote the word *bank* underneath the letters.

Janet's father was beginning to get the sense of the code and asked, "What about *MD* and *TN*? Is it Maryland? Tennessee?"

"Thirty-fourth Street," Janet seemed fixed on that possibility. "Wasn't there a movie about Thirty-fourth Street?"

"Miracle on 34th Street," Janet's father blurted out. "That took place in New York City."

They all looked at one another with sudden recognition. Jack went to a shelf of reference books and brought out a business directory for New York. He leafed through its pages, coming to a halt under "Banks."

"Check this," he said, looking up at Janet. "There's a Midtown Bank on Thirty-fourth Street in Manhattan."

Janet's father added the last part. "Safety deposit *box* 1142."

Back home, later that evening, Janet decided it was time to call Robert's parents and tell them what had been happening. She wasn't quite sure how they would take it but she felt they needed to know. Besides, Jack Knowles had called the Midtown Bank on Thirty-fourth Street in New York and had been told depositor information could not be given out over the phone. If they were to follow up on Jeremy's/ Robert's coded message, Janet would have to fly to New York and meet with the bank officials in person.

Robert's mother and dad came over to the house and they began to discuss all of the pros and cons.

"I'd have to go to New York with our marriage license and Robert's death certificate," Janet told them, "and the truth of the matter is, the money for the trip might turn out to be a total waste."

Mr. Rule turned to his daughter. "You're sure he never mentioned anything you about a bank in New York?"

"You know how Robert was," she replied. "He always wanted to handle the finances and money matters himself. He didn't want to burden me, he said."

Janet picked up the paper Jeremy had written the fateful letters on. She stared at the combination of symbols and shook her head. "Jeremy couldn't have done this by himself," she said. "With all my heart and soul I believe this is a message from Robert."

Mrs. Jentree spoke up. "So do we all, darlin', so do we all."

It was settled. The family agreed to come up with the money for Janet to make the trip to New York. Two days later she was landing at JFK International with their marriage license and Robert's death certificate folded neatly in her purse.

When she arrived at the bank, the manager was both sympathetic and helpful. The signature on the bank papers, Janet recognized immediately as Robert's. According to the date on the rental agreement the safety deposit box had been rented on one of Robert's earlier trips to New York.

It took just a few minutes to get the necessary clearances, and before long Janet found herself standing alone in a small cubicle, Robert's safety deposit box on the shelf in front of her. Just seeing his signature on the papers had brought her emotions right to the edge of her self-control, and her hands trembled as she slowly lifted the lid and looked at the contents.

The first thing she noticed was the money, a small pile of bills in five-, ten-, and twenty-dollar denominations. Her heart skipped a little; maybe her financial problems, at least, would be solved. Alas, that was not to be. A careful count told her there was only $925 there. It would take half that to pay for the trip to New York.

She was about to close the lid when she noticed a piece of paper, neatly folded in the bottom of the box. Janet withdrew the paper, opened it, and started to read. Suddenly she staggered, grasping the edge of the table as she lowered herself into the one chair in the cubicle. What she was holding in her hand was an insurance policy for one hundred thousand dollars. Robert had apparently taken it out on one of his trips to the city. As she read further, two words jumped out at her: *"double indemnity."* In case of accidental death the value of the policy was doubled. Two hundred thousand dollars.

Robert had kept his promise. He had somehow reached out from the grave to make sure his wife and son would be cared for.

Back home in Leesborough, Janet's father and Robert's parents listened intently as she told them what she had found. "Jeremy and I were at the end of our rope," she said, and added, "I know, and God does, too, that Robert's love and his promise, somehow, in some miraculous way, came across from the beyond to save us."

Janet and Jeremy made a special trip to the cemetery a few days later. Janet placed a small bouquet near the headstone, and tucked inside was a note. It was handwritten and folded just once. Anyone passing by could stop and read it. It said simply, *I love you forever, too, my darling.*

There is no doubt in Janet Jentree's mind that the love Robert held for her and their son, Jeremy, somehow penetrated the veil that separates the living from those who have passed on, to rescue them from disaster and despair.

Time, the great healer, has closed the wound, but their love affair continues to this day. Each year, on their wedding anniversary, Janet renews the small bouquet on Robert's grave. And if you look closely you can read the handwritten note she and Jeremy always include. It says: *I LV U 4 F R 2.*

There are those who would tell you that love like Robert and Janet's can only be found in the quiet heart of a small community like Leesborough. But even on the mean streets of the inner city love can find its way. It may be more difficult to come by and certainly more difficult to see, but it's there and it has the same nurturing, healing effect. And isn't it amazing that even though love touches all of us in different ways, the result is invariably the same: love given brings love in return.

CHAPTER 15

MISS MARY'S
HEART

≈≈≈

L EE MARTIN GREW UP IN ONE OF THE TOUGHEST BLACK NEIGHBORHOODS in Dallas. He stuck it out through high school, spent four years in the Air Force, came back to the old neighborhood, and decided he would stay there. Somehow he would find a way to make things work and make the neighborhood better in the process. Lee Martin went to work. He struggled and saved for twelve years and finally bought a struggling auto repair shop.

Marriage to his wife, Marcella, happened later than usual for both of them; they were well into their thirties. When their son, Jimmy, came along he quickly became the center of their lives.

By the time Jimmy was thirteen years old, he had acquired much of his father's ambition and stick-to-itiveness. He had a neighborhood newspaper route and he had, completely on his own, found a retired schoolteacher everyone lovingly called Miss Mary, who was more than willing to spend time with him and give him the benefit of her long years as a teacher. You see, Jimmy Martin wanted to be a writer. Other kids his age were still trying to decide whether they wanted to be policemen or firemen or basketball stars. Jimmy *knew* what he wanted to be. He would be a writer, and Miss Mary found in his youthful ambition that rare combination of determination and intellect that would make achievement of his goal a certainty. Jimmy and Miss Mary had created a very special bond.

The daily routine for Jimmy Martin was as follows: School by eight A.M., home for lunch and a quick trip to Martin Auto Repair for lunch with his dad, then back to school until three P.M. After school he came home, picked up the newspaper saddlebags and his bundle of papers, delivered them, and then stopped by Miss Mary's for an hour of reading James Baldwin or Steinbeck or Shelley. He was usually home for dinner by six, sometimes seven, P.M.

In spite of his schedule Jimmy was carrying a B-plus grade average in school. The only problem seemed to be his parents. They complained frequently that they didn't get to see enough of him. It was all good-natured, of course—both Lee and Marcella were very proud of their son's attitude about hard work and personal effort.

"It wouldn't hurt," his father said at dinner one night, "if you at least brought the bike to a complete stop when you deliver my lunch."

"Yeah," his mother added, "if I'm not close enough to grab you after school all I hear is the door slam behind you."

"Aw, Mom," Jimmy replied, "I'm on a tight schedule."

Marcella laughed and Lee just shook his head, but inside they were bursting with pride. Their son, they were certain, would *earn* his share of the American dream.

But the price of the American dream, on the mean streets of the inner city, comes with its daily risks and perils. On more than one occasion Jimmy had to bring his bike to a halt and wait while rival gangs went at it. Sometimes with fists. Sometimes with cars. Once he had to drop his bike to avoid being hit by a chromed-out Trans-Am screaming out after an old van full of young toughs. The van had splattered beer bottles all over the parked Trans Am and when the boys sitting in the Pontiac gave chase, the driver paid no attention to anyone or anything around him. Jimmy could have been a sack of dirt for all he cared. By the time he got to Miss Mary's that afternoon Jimmy was still a bit shaken.

Miss Mary lived in a small but tidy house in the midst of this neighborhood, and for Jimmy it was a safe and happy haven within the jagged edges of all the anger and evil that surrounded it.

Mary Harris was eighty-two years old. She had taught at the elementary level in the Dallas school system for almost forty-five years before she retired. Miss Mary was more than beloved in the neighborhood. She was an institution. She had never married, but she called thousands of children her own, and her walls were covered with their pictures. Among her former students were business leaders, lawyers, doctors, janitors, ballplayers, nuns, two congresswomen, an astronaut, and a rock superstar. Jimmy, however, would be her first writer.

There was a knock at the door, but before Miss Mary could get up to answer it she heard Jimmy's familiar voice.

"Hi, it's me."

"Well, you come right on in here," Miss Mary sang out. "Come see what I got for you, young man."

Jimmy, at thirteen years of age, towered over Miss Mary's tiny frame, and in the three years he had been stopping by to see her he never tired of helping her out. Jimmy always took time to do whatever lifting and carrying she needed and run whatever errands she couldn't do herself before they settled down to the important business of getting acquainted with the great writers. Jimmy treasured Miss Mary, and she nurtured him as if he were family.

Miss Mary had turned so many children into readers that she had lost count. But Jimmy was special. Not even his mom and dad knew of his ambition to be a writer. He knew his dad expected him to come into the auto repair business with him but Jimmy had other ideas. But, he didn't want to hurt his father's feelings so he just kept it between himself, and Miss Mary. For her part Miss Mary fanned that spark every chance she could. From Steinbeck to Baldwin to Langston Hughes, she opened the wonder of words to him.

Today there were no errands to run, nothing to be lifted or carried. She just urged him to come in and sit down. On the coffee table in front of them was a book. The cover was a dark red moroccan leather.

"That's a little birthday something for you," Miss Mary said, indicating the book.

Jimmy just looked at it. There was an almost reverent expression on this face.

"It's *Selected Poems of Langston Hughes,*" Miss Mary said. "He was not only a great American poet and writer, he was a great African-American poet and writer, like you're going to be someday."

Jimmy picked up the book and turned it over in his hands before opening it very carefully. "But my birthday isn't until January," he protested.

Miss Mary laughed. "I won't tell if you don't," she said.

This would be one of those nights Jimmy didn't get home until seven P.M.

At the Martin home, around six P.M., Marcella looked up from her computer when she heard what she thought was the front door slam. "That you, Jimmy?" she called. "Do me a favor and check the stove. Make sure I set it on low, I don't want the soup to boil off."

There was no answer.

Marcella got up and made a beeline for the living room. "James Ellington Martin," she snapped, "are you playing jokes on me?"

There was still no response. She looked around the living room and poked her head into the kitchen. There was no one there. Marcella started back to her office and felt a cold chill run up her back. As she turned around she saw a picture of Jimmy, his latest school picture, lying on the floor. Somehow it had fallen from the table. The silver frame it was in was probably heavy enough to account for the sound she had heard, but why had it fallen? Carefully she bent down and picked it up. The glass was shattered and would have to be replaced before it could be returned to its former spot.

It was just an accident, she thought, but she couldn't escape the uneasy feeling that had struck her so forcefully when she saw the picture on the floor.

Marcella was sitting on the edge of the couch, still holding the picture, when she heard a similar sound. This time it was the door and Lee and Jimmy came into the living room together.

"Hey, Marcella," Lee said good-naturedly, "it's nice to see you out of your cave." He gave Jimmy a hug and added, "Show your mother what you got."

Jimmy handed the book to his mother, who had to put the picture aside in order to take it. She felt oddly embarrassed and hastily slipped the picture under a pillow, hoping neither of them had noticed it.

"Miss Mary gave it to me," Jimmy said, "for running errands and stuff."

"Well," his mother replied, instantly recognizing the value of the book, "we're going to have to meet this lady friend of yours one of these days."

"You keep saying that," Jimmy replied, "but you're always too busy."

"Hey, I'm not too busy to shoot some hoops," his dad said, slapping him on the shoulder. "You up for it?"

Jimmy looked up at his father and smiled. "I'd really like to, Dad, but I've got a bunch of homework." Jimmy took the book back from his mother and walked out of the room.

Jimmy got his determination from both sides of the family. His mother had started a mail-order business with a secondhand typewriter and a hundred-dollar loan from Lee. Now the typewriter had been replaced by a computer and her business was producing roughly forty percent of the family income.

"Now who's too busy?" Lee called after him.

Marcella took note of her husband's disappointment. Lee really did want to spend more time with his son, it just never seemed to work out for them. She decided a change of subject might be in order.

"Langston Hughes," she said, taking Lee by the arm, "—that's pretty deep stuff for a thirteen-year-old."

"Yeah." Lee looked back over his shoulder toward Jimmy's room. "Our baby's growing up. Every time I look at him it seems like he's a foot taller." He kissed his wife on the cheek and added, "I'm not sure I like him spending so much time with that old schoolteacher."

"You're just jealous," Marcella replied, giving him a punch on the arm.

"You bet I am." Lee's tone was about half serious. "He's got time to do her errands, but he's too busy for a little round ball with his old man." He tried to muster a glare, but it didn't fool Marcella.

"Soup smells great," he said. "I'm going to get washed up."

Lee got up and walked into the bathroom and Marcella went back to the couch and retrieved the picture of her son. Stupid accident, she thought, as she carried it into her office and tucked it away, but for the life of her she couldn't imagine how it could have happened.

Early morning on the first day of October was clear and crisp. For the budding writer the combination of bright sunlight and stinging cold was an invitation to jump right into another exciting day.

For Miss Mary the day began in quite a different way. At ten forty-eight A.M. a neighbor, Madeline Baslin, stopped in for a visit and found Miss Mary sprawled on the living-room floor in a coma. Alone in her tiny home, she had suffered a stroke. If Madeline hadn't stopped by she would have surely died. As it was, the ambulance driver and his partner weren't too sure she'd make it.

By three-thirty in the afternoon Jimmy, completely unaware of Miss Mary's condition, was beginning his usual paper deliveries. His route took him to many of the merchants in the neighborhood, which meant he had to go through the area where the gangs hung out. Most of the time nobody bothered him and he got rid of a lot of papers quickly because the stores were so close together.

Most of the time.

On this particular afternoon, with a bright afternoon sun trying to stave off an early cold snap, Jimmy Martin rode his bike into harm's way. He heard the low growl of the Trans Am's engine and braked to a stop, but this time the car was moving slowly, as if it was tracking someone. The last thing that Jimmy saw was the gun barrel protruding from the partially rolled down window.

At three forty-eight P.M., October first, James Ellington Martin, aged thirteen, the young man who might have picked up the torch passed on from Langston Hughes and James Baldwin, died, an innocent victim of the random violence that plagues our inner cities.

For Lee and Marcella Martin life would never be the same. The lamp that guided their hopes and ambition had been forever dimmed.

Going to work each day, opening up the shop he had worked so hard to own, became nothing more than a habit for Lee. And alone in the silence of her office Marcella often found herself staring at the picture of her son through the shattered lines of the still unrepaired glass.

Miss Mary, of course, had no way of knowing what a fateful autumn day it had been for both herself and the boy she had grown so close to. It puzzled her, and hurt a little, that Jimmy had not come to see her in the hospital, but she put it down to youthful forgetfulness, a girlfriend, perhaps, or a sudden interest in sports. Anyway, as soon as Miss Mary was strong enough to make her way around she insisted on going home. There was a better chance he would come to see her there.

In the months since her stroke Miss Mary had made great progress and, in fact, was doing quite well for herself. She dearly missed seeing Jimmy and said so often, but neighbors, wanting to spare this ill and elderly woman any more heartache, chose not to tell her of Jimmy's tragic death.

Then, one day shortly before Christmas, Miss Mary decided to make an early lunch for herself. She had been getting around her small house with the help of a device that permitted her to walk slowly while still having something solid to lean on.

Mary retrieved a couple of eggs from the refrigerator, then made her way over to the two-burner gas stove. Positioning the walker in front of the stove she turned on the gas and snapped the hand-held igniter she kept near the burners. When it didn't produce a spark, she just reached up for the matches that were always there on a shelf above the stove. She had done this at least a thousand times, but now there wasn't enough strength in her legs to accommodate the reach. Without warning she slipped sideways and as she clung desperately to her walker it tipped with her weight and collapsed beneath her.

Miss Mary crashed to the kitchen floor, unable to move, unable to do anything to alleviate the pain, and unable to reach up and turn off the gas that was rapidly filling her home. The situation was hopeless . . . and deadly.

She didn't know how long she had been lying there, but Miss Mary knew she was in danger and she struggled valiantly to stay conscious. Abruptly she heard the back door open and footsteps coming toward her. With great effort Miss Mary turned her head to see who had come to rescue her. Out of the corner of her eye she caught just a glimpse as a hand reached down and shut off the gas. A pained smile broke over her face.

"Jimmy," she whispered, "Jimmy, I'm so glad you came."

She watched the strong young man step briskly to the window and throw it open and a few moments later she was looking into his smiling face as he picked her up and carried her effortlessly into her bedroom and laid her gently on the bed.

Miss Mary wanted to speak to him, to ask him where he had been, but the ordeal had used up all her strength. She was content to lie back comfortably as Jimmy pulled a cover over her and tucked it under her chin. He touched her forehead briefly, then bent down and kissed her softly on the cheek. Miss Mary saw him walk away as she drifted off to sleep.

She was awakened a short time later by the sound of her neighbor's voice.

"Miss Mary . . . Miss Mary," Madeline shouted frantically, "Miss Mary, where are you?"

Once again this thoughtful friend had stopped by to check on the old woman. When no one answered her knock she came in and immediately detected that faint odor of gas. When she saw the broken walker in front of the stove she began shouting. A moment later her head popped through the bedroom door.

"Oh, Miss Mary," she said with a sigh of relief, "you near scared me to death. What happened?"

The old woman was struggling to find a voice, but eventually she got it out. "I fell in the kitchen," she said in a hoarse whisper, "couldn't get up. Gas was on. Thank God Jimmy Martin came by. He picked me up. Put me in bed."

Madeline pulled a chair up next to the bed and took Miss Mary's hand in hers. Tears glistened in her eyes as she began to speak. "I don't know who it was that came in, Mary"—she struggled to keep her voice calm—"but it couldn't have been Jimmy." Madeline took a deep breath and continued. "We all thought we'd wait till you were better to say anything but . . . the same day you had your stroke . . . Jimmy was shot and killed."

Miss Mary looked at her friend with a mixture of anguish and disbelief. "No," she said, "no, that cannot be. He was here. He saved me." Tears coursed down her aged and weathered cheeks.

At the home of Lee and Marcella Martin the stark, undecorated Christmas tree in the corner did nothing to alleviate the somber mood. After much deliberation they had decided to put something on the tree, just for appearance' sake. Lee stood there, among the boxes of ornaments and decorations, and stared into the green branches, seeing nothing but the echo of some past Christmas.

"I don't even know why we bothered to buy this stupid tree," he said angrily. "There's no Christmas here this year."

Marcella went to him. The burden on her own heart was easily a match for his, but she found the strength to put her arms around him. She held him tightly but his expression never changed.

"At least we tried," she said. "Jimmy would have wanted us to do that."

Lee let an arm fall across his wife's shoulders. They stood there, lost in the quiet, for a long time. This was a house full of emptiness and nothing either of them could imagine would ever change that.

As they stood there in the silence of their shattered dreams, the sound of the telephone was like an explosion.

"Let it ring," Lee said flatly. "I don't want to talk to anybody anyway."

Slowly Marcella released him and turned to answer the phone. Maybe it would help to hear a friendly voice.

By evening Miss Mary was able to move about again and she had decided it was time she got to know Jimmy's parents. Maybe it would help, she thought, if they knew Jimmy was still close by, still helping others.

When Marcella answered the phone, Miss Mary introduced herself and told her exactly what had happened earlier in the day. She was not prepared for Marcella's reply.

"Look," Mrs. Martin snapped into the phone, "I don't know who you are, but I hope you have a nice laugh with your sick little joke."

She slammed the phone down. On the other end there was a loud click and the receiver went dead in Miss Mary's ear.

"What was that?" Lee wanted to know.

"Oh, I don't know." Marcella was fairly shivering with anger. "Jimmy's friend Miss Mary, or somebody saying she was. She said Jimmy was at her place today."

Lee's head jerked around. "Say what?"

"It was just some sicko with a very bad joke," Marcella said. "Forget it."

Miss Mary was troubled and disappointed that her message had been taken as a prank. She was certain that what had happened had had some meaning beyond just saving her life. And she was sure it had something to do with Jimmy's parents. There must be some way to reach them, she thought, and she resolutely picked up a piece of paper and a pen.

Marcella Martin decided she might as well put the decorations away. She put the lids on each box and carried them over to the closet. When she opened the door a package, all neatly wrapped in Christmas paper, fell at her feet. Curious, she put the decorations aside and picked it up.

There was a paper snowman stuck to the front and on it, printed in Jimmy's clear hand, were the words: *To Miss Mary from Jimmy.*

Marcella felt the sudden sting of tears as the pent-up emotion gushed out. "Oh, Jimmy," she cried, "Jimmy, I miss you so." She slumped to the floor, clutching the package to her breast.

Lee leapt to his feet and rushed over to take his wife in his arms. "What is it, Marcie?" And he wept with her, not even knowing why.

They sat there crying in each other's arms for a long time. Finally Marcella handed him Jimmy's gift to Miss Mary. Lee looked at it blankly and tossed it under the tree. "We'll see that she gets it," he said, and gently helped his wife to her feet.

Over the next couple of days the Martins found themselves running into Jimmy's present everywhere. Lee was sure that Marcella was putting it out to remind him that it needed to be delivered before Christmas. Marcella was certain it was Lee who kept moving it about. She would put it under the tree and come out of her office a short while later to find it on the hall table next to the front door. Once Lee came home for lunch and saw it there and tossed it back under the tree himself. When he left to go back to work, there it was by the door again. He just shook his head and walked out.

Then on Wednesday evening Lee came home to find Marcella sitting at the kitchen table. The gift was in the middle of the table and she was trying to read a letter she was holding, but she had to keep stopping to wipe the tears from her eyes.

Lee's reaction was unreasonable and angry. "Here," he growled, "I'll get rid of that thing once and—"

"No!" Marcella reached out quickly and grabbed his hand. "No, we have to take that to Miss Mary tonight. Read this." She handed him the letter.

Lee dropped into a chair and took the letter from her hand and began to read:

Dear Mr. and Mrs. Martin:
Although we haven't met I feel I know you so well. I deeply share the grief of your loss. For, you see, it is my loss too. Over the past few years Jimmy and I grew very close. He became the grandchild I never had. And I believe for him I was the grandmother he never knew. I have no explanation for what happened the other day. I had fallen in my kitchen, unable to get up, and was in danger from the open gas burner. Your son came to me in that moment of need, just as he had so many times in the past. And he saved my life. Impossible as it seems, Jimmy was as real to me as the letter you're holding.

Jimmy is still the sweet and caring boy we knew and loved. He may not be with us on this earthly plane, Mrs. Martin, but I know, without question, his very real spirit is still here, watching over us and spreading his love just as he always did.

Lee looked up from the paper, his eyes wet, his hand trembling. "We've got to go see this Miss Mary, right now," he said.

A short time later the Martins were standing nervously on the front porch of Miss Mary's home. They waited what seemed like a long time for her to answer their knock, but when they saw the walker they understood.

"Miss Mary," Lee began, "we're—"

"Jimmy's parents," Miss Mary finished the introduction for him. "I'm so glad you came, please come in."

By the time Miss Mary closed the door and made her way into the front room, Lee and Marcella had had a moment to take in her "wall of fame."

"My goodness," Marcella said, "are all of these people your students?"

"Yes, all of them," Mary replied.

"That's very impressive," Lee added. Then his eyes fell on the picture of his son. He walked over and touched it. "Too bad Jimmy won't have the chance to live up to his promise," he whispered.

"Lee?" Marcella brought him back to the task at hand. "Don't forget the gift."

Lee handed her the brightly wrapped package.

"We found this at home," Marcella said, handing the package to Miss Mary. "Jimmy must have got it before he got"—she caught herself—"before he died. It's for you."

"Thank you," she said. "Won't you sit down?"

Lee and Marcella smiled and took a seat as Miss Mary began to open the package. Carefully she broke the tape at each end and withdrew an ordinary stationery box. Inside was a sheaf of handwritten papers tied together with a ribbon. On top of the stack of paper was a brief handwritten note. Miss Mary read it and a smile lit up her eyes.

"Mr. Martin," she said. "I think your son has already lived up to his promise." She handed Lee the note. "Read it out loud, why don't you," she said.

"Dear Miss Mary," Lee began,

This is my very first manuscript. I hope you like it. You always told me to write about things I know about, so this is a story about me and my mom and dad, and how much we love each other. I used different names, but if you think it's good enough we can let them read it.

Thanks for everything, and Merry Christmas.

Jimmy.

Miss Mary handed the manuscript to Marcella. "I knew there was more to Jimmy's coming to see me than just saving my life," she said. "He wants you to know that he will always be with you, in your hearts and in your memory, just as you are in his."

The Martins wept openly as Marcella held the precious manuscript close to her breast. Later she had it typeset and bound and today it sits on a bookshelf right next to a leather-bound copy of the works of Langston Hughes.

Lee and Marcella Martin remained Miss Mary's closest friends right up to the day she died. And they never again spoke of Jimmy in the past tense.

The four of them, Jimmy and his parents, and Miss Mary, were all touched by tragedy and bonded by a love unrestricted by this world . . . or the next. But then, that's the power of unconditional love.

CHAPTER 16

THE
THANKSGIVING
TWIN

≈≈≈

I T WAS AN EXCITING DAY AROUND THE GOODRUN HOME. TOM, AN ONLY child, was getting ready for that day young people look forward to and parents dread: he was going away to college.

Not that they didn't want him to go, quite the contrary. Phil Goodrun, Tom's father, and Miriam, his mother, had worked and planned for this day ever since Tom started grade school. It was just that, now it was here, well, they were having a hard time coming to grips with the reality of it. Both of them were certain they had miscounted. It couldn't have been eighteen years since they'd brought him home from the hospital.

The truth of the matter was, Tom was struggling with the idea just a bit himself. Oh, he was excited enough about going, even looking forward to being "his own man," so to speak, but his relationship with his parents had been one of respect and caring. Tom never had to fight with his dad about using the family car, for example, and his dad never had to worry about whether or not Tom would be home at the agreed-upon time. And it was the same with his mother. Theirs was a family relationship of maximum "LFR": Love, Friendship, and Respect.

Tom was dimly aware that something had happened when he was born that prevented his mother from having any other children, and sometimes he regretted that, but all in all theirs was the kind of family that could put most sociologists out of work, if people ever really caught on.

In any case, Tom was too busy just getting everything together to worry about that now. Whatever doubts or fears he might have were buried beneath the excitement of being on his own.

"Mom," he called from the top of the stairs, "what about towels?"

"They're all together for you on the cabinet in the bathroom," she called back, and added, "I'm just taking the rest of your underwear out of the laundry, so leave space."

Tom turned back to his room where two large suitcases were lying open on top of the bed. A shoulder bag loaded with things like his AM/FM/cassette player, his camera, and his favorite music tapes was already zipped up and waiting by the door.

He was still standing there, mentally moving things around, when his mother came through the door with the clean, folded laundry.

"You think I can get everything in two suitcases?" he asked.

"Not if you take everything in the closet," she said, "—that'd take a moving van. I swear, you've got twice as much as you'll need."

"Really?" Tom looked over everything in the suitcases and measured it against what was still in the dresser and the closet. "It doesn't look like I'm taking very much."

"Relax, Tommy." She stuffed the underwear in one corner of a suitcase and headed for the bathroom to get the towels. "If you need anything else I can always send it along. You're letting this packing business drive you crazy."

His mother disappeared out the door, but she was soon replaced by his father.

"You look like you're a little excited about going to school."

"Yeah," Tom said, sitting down between the two suitcases, "it's exciting and . . . a little scary too."

Phil Goodrun laughed and walked over to his son and put a comforting hand on his shoulder. "We're going to miss you around here, you know."

Tom looked up at his father and, in a sudden burst of affection, stood up and threw both arms around him. "I'm going to miss you, too, Dad, you and Mom both."

"I'm certainly glad you added that last part," his mother said, reappearing with the towels.

Tom laughed and both he and his father wiped something from their eyes. Miriam just looked at both of them and smiled.

"Here," she said, handing him the towels, "you finish packing. I'm going to get dinner on." She kissed him on the cheek. "And don't think you're going to get out of here without giving me one of those hugs."

"I can handle it," Tom replied.

"Well, I'll get out of your hair too," his father said, slapping him on the back. "Besides, there might be something she wants me to taste-test."

Tom turned back to the task at hand. He took a deep breath and stuffed the towels in on top of his clean underwear and stood back. That's when he noticed the extra toothbrush. *Now, why did she put that in there?* he wondered, just assuming his mother must have added it. Tom remembered laying his toothbrush out very carefully, along with a belt and the yellow tie with the navy-blue circles. Casually his eye checked for those. They were there, along with an extra belt and the red tie with green accents. He couldn't remember having put those in either.

He was puzzled, but only for a moment. Tom Goodrun was used to this sort of thing. Most of his life it seemed that he had been doing this. He'd get ready for church on Sunday morning, pick out a tie, and when he came back to put it on, there would be two ties for him to choose from. He had decided long ago it was just his mother's or his father's way of telling him to take another look at things. In any event, it was no big deal. He just slammed the suitcases closed and set them alongside the shoulder bag. He was ready to go.

Tom and his parents enjoyed a very special evening together. His mother cooked his favorite fried chicken with baked potatoes and lots of butter and sour cream and afterward they just talked, well into the night.

The following morning, however, things got quickly back to the hectic pace of the day before. Tom jumped out of bed with the first sound of the alarm and was in the bathroom brushing his teeth when he heard the dumb thing go off again. Still frothing at the mouth, he rushed back into his room and shut it off a second time. *Must have hit the snooze button,* he thought, as he walked back into the bathroom to finish getting ready.

He was hauling both suitcases down the stairs, with the carry bag over his shoulder, when his dad came to his rescue.

"Here, let me take a couple of those," he said, lifting the suitcases from Tom's hands. "There's some orange juice on the table for you."

"Thanks, Dad."

Tom detoured through the kitchen, grabbed the glass of orange juice, and slugged it down. He set the empty glass on the table and followed his dad out to the car. They got everything situated in the trunk and walked back inside together.

"Better have a good breakfast before we take off," his father said.

"Oh, no, that's okay," Tom replied. "The orange juice is fine."

"All right, but you'd better drink up. Your mother will be down any second."

Tom looked at the table. There was a glass *full* of orange juice sitting across from the one he had just emptied.

"But . . ." he started to protest, staring at the orange juice. Finally he just shrugged and downed the second glass. His mother must have poured it, he thought; no point in arguing about it. Of course, she was still upstairs and they hadn't been outside long enough for . . . !

In the haste and distraction of the busy morning, Tom dismissed the incidents without serious thought. Besides, he couldn't have explained them anyway. If he had asked, and his mother told him she hadn't come downstairs, it would just have made things more confusing.

The strange double occurrences never seemed to show up at college, and Tom passed the first few months uneventfully. His classes kept him busy, and making new friends also took a fair amount of time. Tom enjoyed both immensely.

He really hadn't planned on going home for Thanksgiving, but this year his mother's birthday also fell during the long holiday weekend. Tom was seriously thinking of changing his plan to stay at school when a lucky turn of events settled the matter for him. One of his newfound friends in the dorm had to cancel his plans to go home and he sold Tom his train ticket for half price. It was just too good a deal to pass up.

With a sudden rush of excitement, and stronger feelings of being homesick than he would ever have admitted to, Tom punched up his parents' number on the phone.

"Hey, Mom, better set an extra place for Thanksgiving."

"Oh, Tom, can you make it after all?"

Tom explained the lucky break on the train ticket and allowed as how, under the circumstances, maybe they could afford it.

"Oh, yes, Tom, yes. In fact your dad and I were just talking today about trying to come up with the money for a ticket for you." She paused. "But we weren't sure how you'd feel about coming back home again so soon, I mean—"

"Mom," he interrupted, "I'd rather be with you and Dad than any-place I know. Just save me a drumstick."

"Don't worry, Tom, we wouldn't think of starting without you."

"If the train is on time, I should be in about two P.M. I'll call you from the station when I get there."

"Oh, if I know your father"—she laughed—"he'll be waiting at the gate."

"Good. That'll save me a quarter." They both laughed and Tom added, "I love you, Mom. Tell Dad I love him too."

Thanksgiving morning Tom arrived at University Station in plenty of time. He didn't want to take any chances of missing the train and he wanted a little extra time to see if he couldn't find a nice card for his mother's birthday. He checked in at the counter, got the gate number, and went directly to the gift shop. It only took him a few minutes to find just the card he'd been looking for. Tom selected an appropriate envelope and took both to the counter.

"Change your mind?" the vendor asked.

"I beg your pardon?" Tom thought he must have missed something.

"About the birthday card?"

"Uh, no," Tom answered, still puzzled, "this is the one I want."

"Yeah, sure." The vendor shrugged. "If you want 'em both it's okay by me."

Tom collected his change and walked away from the counter. *That guy's been working too hard,* he thought. Tom looked around the waiting room for something he could use for a desk so he could write a note on the card. He spotted an empty table over near the shoeshine stand and made his way there. It was one of those stand-up tables designed for people who don't have the time or the desire to sit down while they eat their hot dog.

He finished the inscription, slipped the card in the envelope, and put that inside one of the zipper pouches in his carry bag. "Perfect," he said to himself, as he started back for the waiting room.

"Hey, boy, how'd you get them shoes so messed up?"

"Huh?" Tom spun around. The shoeshine man was looking right at him. "Are you talking to me?" he asked incredulously.

"Sure! I just give you my best 'hi-shine' and you turn right around and mess 'em up. You're gonna give me a bad name. Come on over here, let me touch 'em up."

Tom just stared at him. *That's a new one,* he thought, as he made his way back to the waiting room. *Probably hit me up for a buck once I'm in the chair.*

He spotted an empty seat that gave him a good view of the announcement board and sat down. The two strange comments were beginning to make him feel a little bit uncomfortable, and he decided to get his mind on something else before they called his train. Tom checked his watch and settled back with one of the books he'd brought from school.

He hadn't read more than two or three pages when a movement

caught his eye. What he saw when he looked over the top of his book made the hair stand up on the back of his neck. There on the other side of the waiting room was a young man, just about his age, who looked exactly like him. Same shirt, same jacket, everything.

As he stared, transfixed by this very unusual discovery, the other young man caught his eye and smiled.

There is an old saying that everyone has a twin somewhere on the face of the earth. As Tom would discover later, however, this was not that kind of happy coincidence.

Tom quickly stuffed the book back in his bag and stood up. The other young man was gone. Tom started to move in the direction he had seen him going and finally spotted him once again, moving through a crowd of people who had just disembarked from another train. It looked like he was heading for the exit. For some reason Tom felt compelled to catch up to him, to ask him his name, where he was from, anything.

Suddenly the public address system blared out: "Train for Bay City and points north, now ready for boarding."

Tom looked at his watch, looked over at the gate, and looked back to where he had last seen his double. Strangely enough, the young man was still standing in the same spot, only now he was looking at Tom, and as soon as Tom caught his eye, he smiled that same enigmatic smile and started toward the exit once again.

Suddenly Tom was seized with a sense of urgency. He threw the bag over his shoulder and hurried toward the mysterious stranger, dodging other passengers and doing his best to keep his target in sight. He was gaining, but at the main entrance to the station the young man stopped and turned back to look at Tom one more time. Tom was close enough now to see that, except for a small birthmark just above his right eyebrow, he was looking at a perfect mirror image of himself. Surprised, he stopped, frozen in his tracks. Then there was that smile again and the young man disappeared through the door.

When the boy moved it seemed to free Tom and he lunged for the door. When he burst through into the street, his double was nowhere to be seen. Frantically he surveyed the street in both directions. Off to his right there was just a glimpse of the other boy disappearing around the corner.

Tom shouted and raced to the corner at top speed, but when he got there his double had vanished completely. Tom sagged and let the travel bag slip from his shoulder. For some reason he felt a huge sense of disappointment. Why, he wasn't sure, but he was disappointed nonetheless.

The shrill whistle of the train as it pulled away from the loading platform brought him back to his senses. Tom spun around and raced back inside. He got to his gate just in time to see the last car of the train pull away from the station.

For the moment at least, Tom's mysterious double was forgotten. The train and his precious half-price fare were gone for good. More importantly he had promised to be home. His parents would be waiting for him, counting on him to be there. He couldn't let them down.

That left him just one choice: the old, reliable thumb. He took a lined yellow notepad from his pack and wrote BAY CITY across it in bold letters. By the time he got to the main road out of town he was already a half hour behind schedule.

Luck was with him, though. The second car that saw his sign stopped and picked him up. Now if luck stayed with him he'd make it home in time after all.

Just about an hour down the road Tom would discover how truly lucky he really was.

Tom was napping when he felt the car begin to slow down. When he looked up he could see two patrol cars, lights flashing, stopping all the cars up ahead.

"Wow," Tom said, "I wonder what happened up there?"

"Don't know," the driver replied, "but I'll see if I can find out."

It took them a few minutes to get up to the roadblock, but Tom noticed everyone was pulling onto a side road or turning around and heading back. *Oh, boy,* he thought, *maybe I should have just stayed at school.*

"What's the problem, officer?" the driver asked, as he rolled down his window.

The police officer bent down so the driver could see him. "Bad accident up there," he answered. "Where you headed?"

"Bay City."

The officer pointed off to his right. "You'll have to detour up Twelve here," he said, "then pick up Highway Twenty at Alden. Shouldn't slow you up too much."

"Thanks."

He was about to roll up his window when Tom leaned over and asked, "What happened?"

"Eighteen-wheeler decided to tangle with the train out of University Station." The officer shook his head. "We've got some folks hurt pretty bad up there." He stood up and waved the car on.

The driver of the car finished rolling up the window and turned slowly onto State Road 12. "Wasn't that the train you said you missed?" he asked Tom.

"Yeah," he said, softly, "and I'm glad I did."

Tom turned his head and looked out the window. His eye caught a solitary figure standing by the side of the road and he let out an audible gasp. It was his double, smile and all. As the car rolled slowly by, the young man at the side of the road raised his hand in the familiar "thumbs-up" sign. Tom started to roll down the window to get a better look, but as the glass descended the boy disappeared.

"Something wrong?" the driver asked.

"No," Tom answered, slowly, "no, nothing is wrong."

Bay City is not a large town, and the driver was kind enough to take Tom right to his home. He retrieved his bag from the backseat, thanked his benefactor profusely, and started for the front door. He wasn't more than ten feet up the walk when the door burst open and both his mother and father came rushing toward him.

"Tom, thank heavens you're here." His mother threw her arms around him and broke into tears.

His dad relieved him of his bag, and tried to get an arm around him, too, but he didn't have much success.

"I went to the station to wait for you," he said. "They told me the train had been in a wreck, some people hurt bad. What happened? How did you . . . ?"

Tom turned to his dad and threw his arms around him. "You're not going to believe it," he said. "I'm not sure I do."

The three of them made their way back inside. Phil set Tom's bag at the foot of the stairs and they walked into the dining room. The table was set for three, but dinner was still in the kitchen, waiting for the family to be together again.

"Mmmmmmm, sure smells good in this house," Tom said, sitting at his accustomed place at the table.

Phil and Miriam took their places and waited.

"What is it we won't believe, Tom?" his father asked.

"Yes," Miriam added, "why weren't you on that train?"

"Well, I just sort of missed it." Tom looked from one to the other and realized he was going to have to tell them everything, just the way it had happened.

"It was really weird," he continued. "I was waiting, reading a book. Then I saw this kid on the other side of the station. He was my age, dressed in exactly what I'm wearing and"—he searched their faces again—"he looked enough like me to *be* me."

Tom caught the look that passed between his mother and father, but

they didn't say anything; so he continued unfolding his story. "And where the police had the road closed off, well, I saw him again. I mean, I know it sounds crazy, but it was the very same guy."

His mother was getting very uncomfortable and Tom decided maybe it was time to change the subject. "Oh, I almost forgot," he said, jumping up from the table. "I got you a card . . . for your birthday."

Tom walked out into the hallway and returned with the card he had picked up at the train station. "Here," he said, handing her the sealed envelope. "It isn't much, but I couldn't forget your birthday."

"Oh, thank you, sweetheart." she stood up and gave him another hug. "I'll just check this out and then get dinner on the table. After all, it is Thanksgiving, and we have a great deal to be thankful for."

Miriam opened the envelope, extracted the card, and began reading. Suddenly her smile faded and a tiny cry escaped her lips.

"What?" Tom was stunned. "What is it?"

His father jumped to his wife's side and took the card from her trembling hand. He glanced down at it and registered nearly as much surprise as Miriam had. Slowly he helped her back to her chair.

"This boy you saw today," his father said "—you say he looked exactly like you?"

"Well, yeah"—Tom was still shaking from his mother's reaction to his card—"Except for one thing."

"And what was that?"

"He had a brown spot, like a birthmark, right here." Tom placed his finger at a spot just above his right eye.

"Oh, Phil, it couldn't be." Tears were running down his mother's cheeks, and Tom was on the edge of panic.

"What is it? What's going on here?" he cried.

"Tom, why don't you sit down." His father walked back to his own chair. "There's something we have to tell you." He paused and stared down at the card, as if he couldn't quite believe his eyes. Finally he looked up at Tom. "Maybe we should have mentioned this before, but, well, it just didn't seem necessary." Phil Goodrun took a deep breath. "When you were born," he went on, "you had a twin, a brother. You looked exactly alike, except he had a birthmark over his right eye." Phil reached out and took Miriam by the hand. "We named him Ted, but he only lived a few days."

His mother took the card back and looked at it again and a wonderful light seemed to come into her eyes. "We never wanted to burden you with our grief, so we just didn't mention it."

"But I still don't . . ."

"Look at your card," she said, handing it to him.

There, beneath the birthday salutation he had so carefully written, was his name, just as he had written it . . . and another name scrawled beneath his in a different hand. . . . It said, *Ted.*

Tom looked up at them, understanding beginning to filter into his mind. "He was looking out for me today. My brother, Ted, I mean. He saved me from being on that train."

The room was filled with silence as each member of the family sought to capture what had happened and bring it into their own hearts.

At last Tom stood up and walked back to the wall where the unused chairs were placed. "Do you mind?" he asked, moving one of the chairs up to the table, next to where he always sat.

"No, son, not at all," his father said, wiping tears from his eyes.

Miriam put the card back in the envelope and disappeared into the kitchen. A moment later she returned with another place setting and arranged it carefully in front of the empty chair.

For the Goodrun family, Phil, Miriam, Tom—and Ted—it was indeed a Thanksgiving to remember. And to this day, on Thanksgiving and every family holiday, there is always one extra chair and one extra place setting at the Goodrun family table.

Tom didn't even have to know he had a brother for this marvelous miracle to work in his life, he simply had to be willing to share the love. And once again we are reminded that the veil between this world and the next is very thin. How thin? Perhaps only the thickness of your own belief or your own personal need.

The Goodruns tell me, though, that there are still some people who come to their home on these special occasions who actually believe that chair is empty.

PART V

RELIGION
AND MIRACLES

≈≈≈

As THE PRECEDING CHAPTERS HAVE AMPLY DEMONSTRATED, WONDERFUL things happen to people who do not claim to be particularly religious or have any particular religious affiliation. It is impossible, however, to separate the idea of miracles from some sense of divine intervention.

Perhaps it is because the best-known miracles are those that are associated directly with religion: Moses parting the Red Sea and bringing manna from heaven, Christ healing the lepers or feeding the multitude. Mention the word *miracles* in almost any setting and these are the things that jump immediately to our mind. Indeed, the miracles of Christ's birth, His life, death, and resurrection are probably the most widely acclaimed miracles of all time.

Given the historic veneration of these and hundreds of other miraculous events recorded in religious literature, and accepted by millions of people all over the globe, it would seem facetious at best to ignore the role religion plays in our understanding of miracles and other wonders.

In our own era news stories and investigations from across the country and around the world continue to bring us reports of miraculous events at religious sites and shrines. Hundreds, even thousands, tell of witnessing holy visions, weeping icons, and bleeding statues. There are, even today, startling stories of miraculous healings and instantaneous cures. It simply does not seem possible that they could all be hoaxes or delusions.

These final chapters suggest rather strongly that they could not. As always, however, you must judge for yourself. For many readers these stories will serve simply as a reminder of events they have heard about, or are still hearing about in newspapers or on television. After all, we don't have to go back in time very far to make these discoveries. Some are as current as yesterday's headline, and as near as our own backyard.

In fact, when word got out that I was preparing this book and TV series on miracles and other wonders a very strange thing happened. I began receiving a wide assortment of story suggestions, photographs, and even videotapes that show an amazing variety of phenomena.

CHAPTER 17

THE WEEPING
CHRISTUS

T HIS STORY TAKES PLACE IN THE HOUSTON SUBURB OF BELLAIRE. A TYPI-
cal Texas family, that does typical Texas things, lives there. Dad is a
doctor of veterinary science and also works as an inspector for the
USDA; Mom runs a successful barbecue restaurant, which is just
about as "Texas" as you can get; and their son is a typical young teenager, who spends as much time as he possibly can playing baseball or
basketball.

Along with about three hundred other families they attend St.
Mark's Church on Mulberry Lane.

This is the Ayoub family. They are Egyptians who discovered that
America and its people do, in fact, open their arms and their hearts to
everyone. Tharwat, the veterinary doctor, and Nahed, the barbecue
entrepreneur, emigrated to this country from Egypt fifteen years ago.
And thirteen-year-old Isaac is their ballplaying, pizza-loving Ameri-
can-born son.

But more than heritage distinguishes the Ayoub family. Two events
in recent years have rocked their lives.

In 1989 a series of tests at the Texas Children's Hospital in Houston,
Texas, confirmed that their son Isaac had contracted a life-threatening
illness, lymphocytic leukemia.

Under the supervision of his primary-care physician, Dr. Atef
Rizkallah, Isaac started chemotherapy treatments and over time began
to show steady but slow progress. In early December of 1991 an appointment was made with Dr. Rizkallah to see Isaac for treatment of a

severe sore throat. The doctor immediately feared the leukemia, which had been responding to treatment, had reversed course.

Dr. Rizkallah brought Isaac in and ordered a full blood workup. Much to his surprise they could find no traces of the leukemia.

In cases where this illness responds to treatment at all, it usually takes about five years. But it had only been three years since Isaac's initial diagnosis. It was more than just a remarkable occurrence to Dr. Rizkallah, it was, to use his own words, "nothing short of miraculous."

What had changed? What was different about Isaac Ayoub? What could have brought about the sudden apparent cure?

Isaac's family and friends, and hundreds of strangers who have visited the quiet suburb of Bellaire, believe it is a commonly available portrait of Jesus Christ that hangs on the bedroom wall in the Ayoub family home in Houston.

Why?

This particular portrait, most often in a standard eight-by-ten size, can be seen almost anywhere. It is a "bust" portrait, with the Savior looking off to the viewer's left. The long auburn hair and beard are instantly identifiable. Hundreds of thousands, possibly millions, of prints of this particular portrait have been made. What makes this one so unusual?

Simply this: on November 11, 1991, this portrait, a gift from a family friend, began to weep. Not just a drop or two, mind you; the surface of the picture was virtually leaking. Oily, tearlike drops covered the front. Isaac's mother recalls the event that started it all.

"My son was home sick," she said, "lying on my bed. Suddenly he called out to me, almost frightened."

Isaac remembers that day very well also: "I got up from the bed," he declared, "to get something from the table below the picture of Jesus. I looked up and His eyes moved. Then I saw a hand, Jesus' hand, reach out toward me."

Mrs. Ayoub recalls, "I went right away to the room and there were tears coming from the eyes. I touched the picture and my finger was wet, like oil. There was no reason why it should do this."

Perhaps more astonishing, the weeping has continued now for months. There's so much liquid oozing from the portrait, a holder of cotton batting had to be situated below the picture to absorb all the fluid.

In the months since the phenomenon first began, thousands of people, hundreds a day, have flocked to the modest home in this very ordinary neighborhood, to witness the weeping portrait. People have come from as far away as Florida, Georgia, Colorado, and many other states, as well as some foreign countries.

The pope of the Coptic Church, the Christian sect in which the Ayoubs are members, sent Bishop Tadros all the way from Cairo to examine the portrait. Understandably he arrived with considerable fanfare.

The picture was removed from the wall and inspected. The front of the portrait was wiped dry and they waited. Soon the tears began to flow again. Local religious authorities asked Mrs. Ayoub to donate the weeping portrait to be put on display in St. Mark's, the church where they attend services. Mrs. Ayoub was reluctant.

"I felt it was special," she said, "a gift that had cured my son. I was afraid to move it. Also," she continued, "I thought if we moved it, it would stop weeping."

While her reluctance may, at first, arouse a skeptic's suspicion about the authenticity of the weeping Jesus, what happened next startled even the most devout believers.

Mrs. Ayoub hung other portraits of Christ on the same wall with the original picture. Amazingly, after a short time, they, too, began to weep. And visitors who came to witness the phenomena and pray in the former bedroom that had now become something of a shrine, also brought portraits to place in the room. In many instances these, too, duplicated the weeping.

What is perhaps even more amazing, others, besides Isaac, have reported miraculous healing experiences. And the people witnessing these events are not exclusively members of the Coptic Orthodox faith.

Houston resident and lifelong Catholic Barbara Cashiola told me that she herself witnessed the crying.

"I'm totally convinced it's a miraculous event," she said. "I've been back many times by myself and with others. The portrait has continued to weep."

Still reluctant to move the original portrait, Mrs. Ayoub, in a special ceremony, donated a *second* portrait to St. Mark's Church. One that she had hung for a time next to the original. And as this book is being written . . . yes . . . the donated portrait, on display for all to see, is still weeping.

What began as a very private experience for one young boy and his family has spread far beyond the confines of a Houston suburb and far beyond what anyone could have guessed.

"A lot of people who come," Mrs. Ayoub said, "believe, once they get to the room and see. A lot of them cry. A lot of them feel the presence of God. A lot of them feel peace."

What a remarkable miracle that must be.

But what could possibly account for the weeping portrait in that suburban Houston home? Some unknown phenomenon? Mass religious hallucination, perhaps? Could the cures of thirteen-year-old Isaac, and reportedly others, have some less fantastic explanation?

Ultimately you must decide for yourself. But remember, thousands of people from Texas and across the country—indeed, around the world—have seen and experienced something extraordinary with their own eyes. For them there is no question. They have witnessed a true miracle.

CHAPTER 18

THE VIRGIN
OF GUADALUPE

≈≈≈

Pinto Lake is a sleepy, out-of-the-way public park near Watsonville in Santa Cruz County, California. Kids play here, dogs run free, and an occasional Frisbee slices through the air. Not at all a typical setting for a religious shrine. In the past even a busy Saturday would bring not more than a few dozen cars to this spot.

But now the quiet days of Pinto Lake Park are over, thanks to Mrs. Anita Contreras Mendoza, a cannery worker from nearby Watsonville.

And what did Mrs. Mendoza do to create all of this attention? Actually, all she did was kneel to pray on a quiet summer afternoon. Seeking a corner by herself to offer up her daily prayer, she knelt in front of an ordinary oak tree in a back corner of the park. A tree on which thousands say they can now see the distinct shape of the Virgin of Guadalupe. That is the unique bowed head of the mother of Christ as she appeared in 1531 on the robe of a Mexican peasant.

The image is formed in a distinct pattern of dark and light bark on the old oak tree before which Mrs. Mendoza bowed her own head.

The events began to unfold shortly before noon in June of 1992. But let's let Mrs. Mendoza tell it in her own words.

"I knelt to pray about eleven-thirty that morning, when a gust of wind came and moved all the trees. At one point a beam of light hit the tree. The Virgin of Guadalupe appeared and for a moment I saw her face. Then she disappeared, leaving behind her image in the bark of the oak tree."

Mrs. Mendoza experienced the vision of the Virgin twice over two days. And the word spread. As many as ten thousand visitors have since come to visit the site on a single weekend.

A modest and humble miracle, perhaps, but then these are a modest and humble people. Father Mike Miller of the local Catholic parish sees it as fitting that such a vision should appear for them.

"The Virgin Mary's pattern, with the famous apparitions, like Fatima or Lourdes or Guadalupe, has been to go to the people who are disenfranchised, that are poor, that are miserable, that are not at the center of things," he said. "We believe like a mother, she seeks out the children that need her the most and reassures them."

Indeed, if a community ever needed a miracle it is this one. Due to drought and recession Mexican-American farm workers are unemployed in extraordinary numbers in this part of the state. Then, of course, there was the earthquake. Neither the town of Watsonville nor its people have fully recovered from the effects of the Loma Prieta earthquake of 1989. Economic gloom and personal despair have been longtime residents of this community.

The appearance of images such as this always invites debate, but there is little disagreement about the large number of people who have seen this image or the deep emotions they have experienced.

Ken Kramer, a professor of religious studies, told me, "I would never discourage someone from saying that it was the Virgin Mary. In fact, I would encourage this woman in her faith, because after all there are far too few things in this world now that people can put faith and hope in."

As people began to visit the site many recounted strange happenings. We interviewed a number of these people.

Basilisa Lopez told of finally being able to throw away his cane.

"After seven years," he said, "I can walk on my own. It was My Lady. God has given me my wish."

Olaya Hernandez is convinced, beyond any shadow of a doubt, that the Virgin of Guadalupe has a definite purpose for being in this particular spot.

"To me it is real," she says, "and I do feel, when I pray and pray, I do feel the presence. I believe the Virgin is here to protect us and for us to get together and pray."

Mary Lee Scott echoes those sentiments: "She's just telling this world to shape up. If we don't, something's going to happen, and I believe this."

Esther and Abel Dominguez drove three hours to visit the Watsonville site. Abel had injured his lower back and could hardly walk.

"He had trouble coming up," Esther said, "but now he's going up and down that hill."

Father Miller sees the wisdom of God in this remarkable appearance. "The Virgin Mother has chosen a good place to give reassurance to people who need to see her," he said, "and they feel like somebody is sending them love. God has a language he uses with each person."

Whatever it was that happened here, this once anonymous, nondescript oak tree has been turned into an impromptu shrine. Bouquets of flowers, rosaries, pictures of children, the elderly, the sick, are all left here by the faithful.

There is no question that a miracle of hope has entered the lives of these people. For many this humble vision, by way of a colored patch of bark on one of God's otherwise very ordinary oak trees, is miracle enough.

CHAPTER 19

THE MAKING
OF A SAINT

≈≈≈

O NE OF THE MOST DIFFICULT THINGS THERE IS IN THE ECUMENICAL world is to be declared a saint by the Catholic Church. During this entire century only eleven times have the strict requirements been met. One of these requirements, indeed a key requirement, is that miracles must be *proven* to have occurred in the person's name who is proposed for sainthood.

On May 31, 1992, the official announcement was made which acknowledged that a miracle had indeed occurred. And it happened, not in some distant foreign land, but right here in America, in Santa Monica, California.

On that day, in St. Peter's Basilica in Rome, Pope John Paul II spoke the Latin words: "We declare Blessed Claude to be among the saints."

With those words a French Jesuit priest joined a very select few. He was recognized by the Roman Catholic Church in the rite known as canonization. Claude de la Colombière, a French Jesuit priest who died in 1682, had attained sainthood.

Blessed Claude's route to that exalted position had begun more than two years earlier here in the United States at Santa Teresita Hospital in southern California. The miracle that was responsible for raising Blessed Claude to sainthood happened to a Jesuit father by the name of John Houle.

Father Houle was a very sick man.

"I had been diagnosed as having terminal pulmonary fibrosis," he said, and added, "At the end of February 1990 I was on my deathbed and had been administered the last rites of the church."

Everyone around Father Houle knew the end was imminent. A Dr. Newberger had been working with Father Houle and described his condition for us.

"On Friday the twenty-third he was unconscious, as he had been on and off for the previous two weeks. He was hooked to oxygen and had very labored breathing. Father Houle was clearly in the last stage of life. None of the doctors gave him a chance of surviving more than several days, perhaps hours."

"On Monday morning he was not only conscious, he was fully awake, cheerful, sitting on the side of his bed. I can state unequivocally his lung condition was cured. There's only one word for his medical recovery: *miraculous.*"

So what happened between Friday afternoon and Monday morning that made Father Houle's terminal respiratory illness miraculously recede? Father Houle and others around him say it began with the prayers of his close friend and fellow Jesuit father, Francis Parrish.

Father Parrish's help, as you might expect, came in the form of prayer, but as Father Parrish tells it, very specific praying.

"Instead of praying to several saints for Father Houle's recovery," Father Parrish reported, "I prayed only to Father de la Colombière, also a Jesuit. Also I blessed Father Houle with a relic of Blessed Claude, a remnant of one of his sacrament robes. When I left his hospital room I told a small group of relatives and friends that he was going to be all right. I don't know how, but I knew it. The next time I saw Father Houle, he was sitting up in bed, slicing an apple to eat. I was relieved, but not at all surprised."

Father Parrish immediately began assembling the medical evidence about Father Houle's extraordinary recovery. He was convinced a true miracle had occurred and that the prayers to Blessed Claude had been responsible.

But it would take proof, overwhelming proof, to convince church officials in Rome that a miracle had indeed taken place.

Bishop John Ward was in charge of the investigating team that documented the cure for the required miracle. It was an arduous process and would go on for many months.

"With doctors' reports, X-rays, various signed statements and declarations," Bishop Ward declared, "we sent off to Rome a stack of papers about a foot high. It was a very thorough process. The Catholic Church does not hand out sainthood readily."

Church headquarters in Rome found the case to be most convincing. French Jesuit priest Claude de la Colombière became just the eleventh person in more than ninety years to be named a saint. And Father Houle's reaction to being a part of these historic developments . . . ?

"It's been a very humbling experience," he stated. "I have another gift of life. It's a mystery, but I am very grateful for the added days and maybe years."

CHAPTER 20

THE BEATRICE, NEBRASKA, MIRACLE

≈≈≈

GOING TO WEEKLY CHOIR PRACTICE AT THE WEST SIDE BAPTIST CHURCH in Beatrice, Nebraska, was the next thing to a habit for the twelve regular members of the choir. Over the years Wednesday night had been set aside religiously (no pun intended) for the group to meet. Other responsibilities were put off and few, if any, other chores, errands, or requests were permitted to interfere.

The regimen was so strict, according to Karen Paul, one of the choir members, that "if you tried to figure the odds on what happened, you couldn't do it."

When he learned of the event even Sheriff John Beech's first reaction was "There probably aren't enough ambulances in the county to handle it."

But we're getting ahead of the story.

The date was Wednesday, March 1, 1950, seven-thirty P.M. Everybody in Beatrice, Nebraska, still, forty-five years later, remembers the time and day. At that precise moment on that day, as a result of a gas leak, the West Side Baptist Church violently exploded.

"What was left," according to choir member Harvey Ahl, "was matchsticks. A person couldn't have survived. The whole thing was demolished."

Herb Kipf, another member of the "miracle" choir, says, "Folks around here still talk about it. We've had people come from as far away as Japan to look into this."

Some choir members, like Karen Paul, now have grandchildren. Karen has seven of them and she says, "When each one arrived I thought back to that Wednesday, March first, and how close they came to never being here."

Ladona Vandegrift still gets tears in her eyes when asked about it. "When something like this happens," she asserted, "you don't just dismiss it. It forces you to ask some pretty deep questions."

Some readers will remember the incident these longtime residents of Beatrice, Nebraska, still talk about. It was headline news in papers from coast to coast, and it is a case study of a miracle if there ever was one.

Usually on Wednesday evenings most of the choir members would show up a little early. Nobody was ever late—except on Wednesday evening, March 1, 1950.

Sadie Estes recalls that she and her sister were late because they couldn't get the car started. But being diligent, they called another choir member, Ladona Vandegrift, for a ride.

"Usually, at time for choir practice," Ladona told me, "I'd set aside what I was doing and leave. But I had a homework problem I was stuck in the middle of, and I was just determined to get it solved."

Another choir member, Dorothy Wood, found her normal routine upset as well.

"My friend Lucille was also in the choir," she remembers. "We'd always walk over to practice together. But she started listening to a radio program that wasn't going to be over till seven-thirty, so I decided I'd wait with her."

Herb Kipf had an even flimsier excuse: "I had finally gotten around to writing an important letter," he said. "I'd been putting it off and the time just got away from me."

Rev. Walter Klempel, pastor of the church, had no better reason for being late than the fact that his watch was slow. The only thing that puzzled him was that his watch was always right on the button. He might have been more accurate than he knew when he said, "For no earthly reason I can explain, that night, March first, my watch was running five minutes slow."

Everybody in town knew that the choir met in the church on Wednesdays at seven-thirty, so when he got the news of the explosion Sheriff John Beech's first thought was "I was going to be counting bodies. It was just a matter of how many."

The natural gas leak in the basement of the church was ignited by the furnace at precisely seven-thirty P.M. The building's furnace was located exactly beneath the choir loft.

Yet, of the twelve members of the choir scheduled for the practice that night, not one was in the church when disaster struck. Imagine the odds. Every single person who was supposed to be there was inexplicably delayed, if only for five minutes.

The choir director, the church pianist, the pastor, his wife, eighteen tardy members of the group in all. Everyone with a valid, if minor, excuse. Twelve people who, on just about any other Wednesday in their memories, would have been in their places in the choir loft and would have died amid the splintered ruins of the exploding Beatrice Baptist Church.

And now, over forty years later, the bounty of this miraculous happening is still very much with us. The children and grandchildren who would have never come into the world have instead grown up to serve their families, their community, and the nation.

Ladona Vandegrift probably best expressed the feelings of all the choir members, who look back on that fateful day with hearts filled with gratitude.

"From what we've all become since, from what we've added to the community, and from the loving families we've been part of, it's plain and simple: something extraordinary happened here. All of us knew, absolutely knew, that being spared from that disaster was not some wild coincidence. We knew exactly what it was."

It is something very special to contemplate. Eighteen different people were delayed, all for minor reasons, and the explosion that would have killed them all . . . missed them all. It's plain to see this little corner of the world called Beatrice, Nebraska, is smack dab in the middle of the kingdom of miracles.

And isn't it encouraging to know that a lifesaving miracle can be brought about by something simple as a watch . . . that runs just five minutes slow.

CHAPTER 21

A RELUCTANT
FAREWELL

≈≈≈

As I come to the last chapter of this book, it is with a feeling of regret. I know that miracles happen every day to people just like you, and I get immense pleasure from sharing these wonderful stories.

Some miracles may lack the high drama of most of the events I have presented here, but nevertheless they provide the punctuation that gives clarity and meaning to the continuing story of life as we live it every day.

On the most ordinary of days in the most typical of places events can conspire to achieve the most miraculous of purposes. Before I leave let me share just a few examples with you.

This happened to a young woman named Lucille Harper.

It was a snowy day in December and Lucille was coming back from an errand just up the street from her home. Her five-year-old was playing in the snow on the driveway at a neighbor's house. As she came up she could see a delivery truck parked in the driveway and it was starting to roll backward, straight at her boy. Lucille took in the entire situation in just a matter of seconds and realized that she could reach the truck faster than she could get to her son, so that's what she did.

By the time she got to the truck the back wheel was about to roll over him. She braced herself and pushed against the back of the truck. Lucille screamed at her boy to get out, but he was on all fours, panicky and slipping on the ice and snow. There was only one thing she could do and miraculously she did it. Lucille shoved the truck forward a few feet so her son could crawl clear.

By this time some of the neighbors saw what was happening and came running, but by then it was all over. The boy was safe. One of the neighbors jumped in and set the parking brake on the truck. The entire episode had lasted less than two minutes.

But what a miracle.

You see, Lucille only weighs about a hundred pounds. The truck was fully loaded and was parked on an incline in the driveway. And last, but by no means least, the concrete was wet and slippery from the snow.

"You could have offered me a million dollars the next day to push that truck up the drive," Lucille declared, "and there's no way I could have done it. Whatever strength I had to move that truck didn't come just from me, I can tell you that."

Lucille doesn't doubt for a minute that there were hands, other than her own, that kept the weight of that truck from crushing her child.

And here's a story that Lillian Miller told me. It's about her father and his dedication to caring for his family. I'll let her tell it in her own words.

"For as long as I can remember my father's hobby was doing handyman chores and fixing up things around our house on Mozart Street in Chicago. One of his rituals was lighting the gas furnace every fall when the cold weather started.

"In October of 1960, about two months after he passed away, a cold spell set in. It was a Sunday afternoon and our family was discussing the weather and if it was time to light the gas furnace. The next thing we know there's a loud banging on the pipes coming from the basement. We just figured it was due to the change in temperature. But we joked to ourselves that it was Dad, happily at work on his chores.

"The next three nights we heard the banging again, even louder than before. It sounded exactly like someone pounding with a wrench. By Thursday the banging on the pipes was so loud, we went down to check on the heater and thought we smelled a gas odor. We called the gas company to have a man come and look at it, which he did the next day.

"He couldn't give us any explanation for the banging on the pipes but he found a major gas leak. He said if we had tried to light the heater there would have been a major gas explosion. We could have all been injured and quite possibly killed.

"After that we all said a prayer of thanks to our father, who we believe had sent us a warning about the dangerous gas leak. Those pipes had never banged like that before, nor have they since. Even after his death we knew that Dad was still taking care of us, doing his chores and looking after his family."

Astonishing isn't it, the way these things just keep happening to people, all over the country and in all walks of life?

Here's one more.

Gerald and Nelda Kelly were used to getting around in their own airplane. Gerald was an excellent pilot and they had been flying together for years.

One weekend they flew to Albuquerque for a few days to visit relatives. When it came time to go home, Gerald did what any good pilot would do: he made a visual check of his aircraft and ran through the entire cockpit check, point by point.

Satisfied that everything was as it should be, Gerald taxied to the runway and got set to take off.

I'll let him pick up the story from there.

"I was in the pilot's seat, with my wife beside me, and for no reason my glasses got all fogged up. I couldn't see a thing. Nelda took my glasses and gave them a good wiping. I put them on again and immediately those glasses fogged right up again. But, and here's the important thing, the lenses weren't misted up, like from perspiration or humidity. They were fogged on both sides.

"Well, it wasn't any use getting tower clearance for takeoff. There was no way I could take off without using my glasses. So I just turned the plane and started taxiing back. But we didn't make it. The engine spluttered out and died. I found out later it was a clogged fuel intake. All I can say is that if we had taken off right away, we'd have been no more than two or three hundred feet off the ground when that engine cut out.

"To this day I have no explanation for why those glasses fogged when they did. But there's no question in my mind that it was some kind of warning that saved our lives. Needless to say, Nelda and I are very grateful."

So far all the people who have had miracles are strangers to you. . . . You don't know them.

It occurs to me that it might create more credibility if you heard about miracles from someone you know very well. I was recently speaking with actor Mickey Rooney and he asked me to pass along to you his story. Here it is in his own words.

"About twenty years ago in Lake Tahoe, I was playing in a room up there with Mac Davis. We were all having an early breakfast. One of the busboys with gossamer golden hair came over to the table and said, 'Are you Mickey Rooney?' I thought he was going to say, 'You're wanted on the telephone,' so I said, 'Yes, I'm Mickey Rooney.' He said, 'Jesus Christ loves you very much.' Nobody else at the table actually saw him. I walked up to the maître d' and I said, 'Where is the youngster with the golden hair?' She said, 'We have no such boy. You can look in the kitchen if you want.' I looked in the kitchen and all over. He wasn't there.

"That was my miracle, my wonder. I was visited by one of Jesus Christ's angels."

Following this wondrous, unexplained visitation, Mickey Rooney, one of the nation's most beloved actors, experienced a resurgence of his career, including a huge Broadway success in *Sugar Babies* and the motion picture and TV series *Black Stallion.* More importantly, it provided him with the strength to face personal challenges that ultimately saved his very life.

Another example of a well-known person experiencing a miracle is that of Della Reese. You know her as a talented actress and wonderful singer. I think you will find this story, in her own words, interesting.

"Because I walked through a plate-glass window, and lost seven pints of blood, and had a thousand stitches, I had an out-of-body experience. They took me directly to the hospital from my home where it happened. The doctors were standing around me deciding there was no need to give me any blood because I had lost so much that I probably wasn't going to be able to be revived.

"I was sitting on top of a cabinet in the postoperative room. I was looking down at these doctors and they were there discussing me. And I was so upset by what they were saying, I came back into my body. Because of that I am here today. I am able to teach today. I am able to preach today. I am able to pastor a congregation. Because of that out-of-body experience I realized I had not done all that I should do and I came back. It was an experience that changed my life."

Though unexplainable forces seem to constantly touch our lives, we should not consider them unnatural. They are a wondrous ingredient in the magnificent mystery we, as human beings, are all a part of, and they are surprisingly common.

Now, there are skeptics and critics, I'm sure, who can find ways to write all of these things off as mere coincidence or self-delusion. To me that speaks of a person who simply doesn't want to believe.

Why, I can't imagine.

My study of miracles, large and small, leads me to the inescapable conclusion that the only thing that prevents these wondrous things from happening more often and to more people is the veneer of skepticism that seems to coat most of our society.

I am reminded of a plaque I once saw prominently displayed on the wall of a social services office. It read: WE DON'T PRAY FOR MIRACLES, WE EXPECT THEM.

And indeed, why shouldn't we? That sweet, generous little lady I was guided to, lying lost and hurt on a dirt road in the mountains of Utah, reached out to whatever power watches over us and simply demanded "fairness." More than that, she expected to get it. I am personally convinced it was that expectation, that faith, if you will, that brought me to her side.

All of us, in my view, have the opportunity, perhaps even the responsibility, to call on that same power, especially in the service of others. Denying that it exists, or that it can help, or that it *will* help, is, it seems to me, just about the only thing that can prevent miracles from occurring in a person's life.

A seventeenth-century philosopher by the name of Pascal wrote something with which I find it very easy to agree. He said: "Belief is a wise wager. If you gain, you gain all; if you lose, you lose nothing."

I am more than willing to confess that my investigation of the events depicted in this book has given me a strong foundation of belief. And I should point out again that the miracles and wonders that fill these pages represent only a fraction of those that are available to the interested investigator.

Beyond these investigations, however, my own personal experiences have erased any doubt there may ever have been in my mind.

Miracles do happen. They are an almost daily occurrence, and I am persuaded that they can happen to all who are willing to open themselves up to this very real *probability*.

It doesn't seem that there are any rules to follow or requirements that must be met before a miracle can take place, but it does appear that these marvelous and miraculous phenomena happen most often to those who are willing to reach out and seek such help in a spirit of love and service.

Pascal was right, belief *is* a wise wager, but that doesn't take it nearly far enough. Belief is also a call to action, a conviction, an expectation that requires something more than just a passive awareness that miracles exist.

Reach out and gather them in.

By the way, if you are one of those fortunate people who have had a miraculous event happen to you, I would like to hear about it. Please write to me.

Chuck Sellier
Miracles and Other Wonders
P.O. Box 529
Baker City, Oregon 97814